# 40 Short Walks in

# SUSSEX

D1369210

Produced by AA Publishing
© AA Media Limited 2011

Researched and written by
Martin Andrew

Additional material and walks
by Nick Channer (updated by Nick Channer,
David Hancock and Tim Locke)

Commissioning Editor: David Popey
Series Management: Sandy Draper
Series Design: Tracey Butler
Copy-editor: Ann F Stonehouse
Proofreader: Pam Stagg
Picture Researcher: Liz Stacey
Internal Repro and Image Manipulation:
Sarah Montgomery
Cartography provided by the Mapping
Services Department of AA Publishing
Production: Lorraine Taylor

Published by AA Publishing (a trading name
of AA Media Limited, whose registered office
is Fanum House, Basing View, Basingstoke,
Hampshire RG21 4EA; registered number
06112600)

 This product
includes mapping
data licensed from the Ordnance Survey®
with the permission of the Controller of
Her Majesty's Stationery Office. © Crown
Copyright 2011. All rights reserved.
Licence number 100021153.

A04616

978-0-7495-6909-9
978-0-7495-6921-1 (SS)

Colour separation by AA Digital

Printed by Oriental Press

Visit AA Publishing at theAA.com/shop

A CIP catalogue record for this book is
available from the British Library.

The contents of this book are believed
correct at the time of printing. Neverthele
the publishers cannot be held responsibl
for any errors or omissions or for changes
in the details given in this book or for
the consequences of any reliance on the
information it provides. This does not affe
your statutory rights. We have tried to
ensure accuracy in this book, but things d
change and we would be grateful if reade
would advise us of any inaccuracies they
may encounter.

We have taken all reasonable steps to ens
that these walks are safe and achievable
by walkers with a realistic level of fitness.
However, all outdoor activities involve a
degree of risk and the publishers accept
no responsibility for any injuries caused t
readers whilst following these walks. For
more advice on walking safely see page
The mileage range shown on the front co
is for guidance only – some walks may be
less than or exceed these distances.

Some of the walks may appear in other A
books and publications.

**Picture credits**

The Automobile Association would like
to thank the following photographers,
companies and picture libraries for their
assistance in the preparation of this book

Abbreviations for the picture credits are a
follows – (t) top; (b) bottom; (c) centre; (l)
left; (r) right; (AA) AA World Travel Library

3 AA/W Voysey; 7 AA/L Noble; 10 AA/D
Noble; 20 AA/J Miller; 42/3 AA/J Miller;
48 AA/M Busselle; 66 © Rob Cole
Photography/ Alamy; 73 Photolibrary;
84 © Malcolm McHugh/Alamy; 90 AA/L
Noble; 97 © Linda Kennedy/Alamy; 114
Photolibrary; 120/1 AA/S&O Mathews;
140 © simon Jonathan webb/Alamy.

Every effort has been made to trace the
copyright holders, and we apologise in
advance for any accidental errors. We wo
be happy to apply the corrections in the
following edition of this publication.

*Opposite: Boats in the harbour at*

# 40 Short Walks in

# SUSSEX

# Contents

| Walk | | Rating | Distance | Page |
|------|------|--------|----------|------|

### Rating

Each walk is rated for its relative difficulty compared to the other walks in this book. Walks marked ✚✚✚ are likely to be shorter and easier with little total ascent. The hardest walks are marked ✚✚✚

### Walking in Safety

For advice and safety tips see page 144.

# Introduction

Since April 2010, much of Sussex and parts of eastern Hampshire have had their outstanding landscape qualities recognised. A vast swathe of the county has been promoted from an Area of Outstanding Natural Beauty to a National Park. Now almost all of the Downs and a good deal of the beautiful countryside centred on Midhurst and Petworth rightly stands on a par with, for example, the Peak District or the Pembrokeshire Coast.

An outside visitor would expect the National Park to run from Beachy Head westwards to the Hampshire border solely along the chalk hills of the South Downs, but in fact from Pulborough westward the whole of western Sussex is included. This is mostly Wealden clay and a much more intimate countryside with secluded valleys and sandy soils atop superb heathland. Surprisingly, the headquarters of the Sussex Downs National Park is not in Lewes or anywhere on the South Downs but in this Wealden clay area at Midhurst.

## A Superb Landscape

Sussex is a county of contrasts though and some areas are distinctly under walked, particularly the coastal plain between Littlehampton and the Hampshire border. Within it, of course, is the original county town of Chichester, historic canals, fine coastal scenery including Pagham Harbour and the Chichester Channel, and Sussex's finest parish church bar none, the surprisingly little known Boxgrove Priory.

Much of north eastern Sussex is also recognised as having landscape of superb quality and is within the High Weald Area of Outstanding Natural Beauty. Several of the routes explore this area that ranges from sandstone hills and sandy or poor clay soils of the Ashdown Forest to the river valleys at the east, which have cut wide swathes to produces ridges, often not very high, such as those on which Winchelsea and Rye stand.

Thus it seems that almost all the county is highly regarded as landscape but these walks also show you some of the superb towns. Several were the headquarter towns of the medieval 'rapes' into which Sussex was divided and were based on castles which survive to varying degrees, including Chichester, Arundel, Bramber, Lewes and Pevensey. Others were market towns such as Steyning, Midhurst and Petworth while some were important medieval ports such as the Cinque Port towns of Rye and Winchelsea.

Apart from superb scenery and towns several of the walks show the industrial heritage of the county including the Wealden iron industry and coppiced woodland, although these are far from the oldest industries. There

*Opposite: The Seven Sisters*

were neolithic flint mines on the slopes of Cissbury Ring, for example, but coming to more recent times several of the walks take in Sussex's railway heritage. Working steam railways such as the Bluebell Railway, the Lavender Line and the Kent and East Sussex Railway are among the county's major tourism assets, but some of these walks also follow the equally evocative routes of long lost railways.

The canal age is also represented, both by canalization of rivers such as the Ouse towards Newhaven, but also 'new' canals from the early 19th century. These feature in the walks on the coastal plain around Chichester, the grandly named Chichester Ship Canal and the Portsmouth and Arundel Canal.

Underpinning all this are the parish churches and villages of Sussex – they are a fine collection and of infinite variety – from Boxgrove Priory and Winchelsea to small Downland churches such as Up Marden.

# Using the Book

This collection of 40 walks is easy to use. Use the locator map, see opposite, to select your walk, then turn to the map and directions of your choice. The route of each walk is shown on a map and clear directions help you follow the walk. Each route is accompanied by background information about the walk and area.

## INFORMATION PANELS

An information panel for each walk details the total distance, landscape, paths, parking, public toilets and any special conditions that apply, such as restricted access or level of dog friendliness. The minimum time suggested for the walk is for reasonably fit walkers and doesn't allow for stops.

## ASCENT AND DIFFICULTY

An indication of the gradients you will encounter is shown by the rating ▲▲▲ (no steep slopes) to ▲▲▲ (several very steep slopes). Walks are also rated for difficulty. Walks marked ✚✚✚ are likely to be shorter and easier with little total ascent. The hardest walks are marked ✚✚✚.

## MAPS AND START POINTS

There are 40 maps covering the walks. Some walks have a suggested option in the same area. Each walk has a suggested Ordnance Survey map. The start of each walk is given as a six-figure grid reference prefixed by two letters indicating which 100km square of the National Grid it refers to. You'll find more information on grid references on most Ordnance Survey maps.

## CAR PARKING

Many of the car parks suggested are public, but occasionally you may find you have to park on the roadside or in a lay-by. Please be considerate when you leave your car, ensuring that access roads or gates are not blocked and that other vehicles can pass safely.

## DOGS

We have tried to give dog owners useful advice about how dog friendly each walk is. Please respect other countryside users. Keep your dog under control, especially around livestock, and obey local bylaws and other dog control notices. Remember, it is against the law to let your dog foul in public areas, especially in villages and towns.

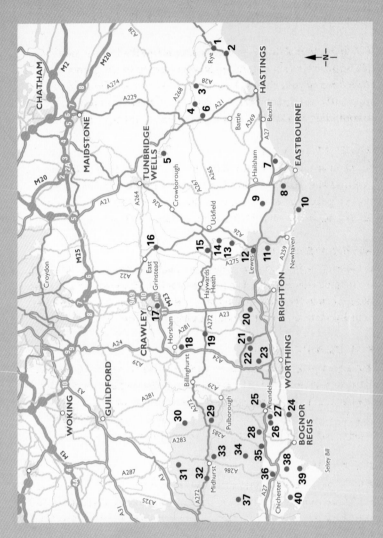

## KEY TO WALKING MAPS

| | |
|---|---|
| ---→--- Walk Route | Built-up Area |
| ❶ Route Waypoint | Woodland Area |
| --- --- Adjoining Path | 🚻 Toilet |
| ⚡ Viewpoint | P Car Park |
| • Place of Interest | ⊞ Picnic Area |
| ⌄⌄ Steep Section | )( Bridge |

# THE TOWN THAT HENRY JAMES LOVED

## A walk to a medieval town with cobbled streets and long views over Romney Marshes

Rye is one of England's most attractive historic towns, set on its ridge with the Rivers Rother, Brede and Tillingham winding round it on three sides and their estuaries forming a natural harbour, called the 'camera'.

### A medieval 'planned' town

Built in the late 11th century, Rye's rectangular grid of streets is still plain to see. Originally held, along with Winchelsea (Walk 2) by Fecamp Abbey in Normandy, Henry III took them over in 1247 and the town became a royal borough and port, becoming one of the Cinque Ports in the 1330s, added as an 'Antient Town' along with Winchelsea.

Throughout the 14th century Rye was raided by the French, and while many timber-framed buildings of the late Middle Ages and Tudor times survive, it is the stone defensive buildings that are reminiscent of the town's more turbulent times. It was a walled town and from this period survives the 1381 Land Gate, through which the walk route passes, and south of the church the Ypres Tower, the town's castle built around 1249. Rye's medieval prosperity and status is reflected in the remains of two friaries and, of course, in its fine parish church of St Mary. All went well until the harbour began to silt up in Tudor times and it became more a prosperous market town with much rebuilding and re-fronting of the old timber houses in the 18th century.

### An American in Rye

One of the best of the 18th-century houses is Lamb House west of the church. A slate plaque on the high garden wall fronting West Street commemorates the novelist brothers E F and A C Benson who lived here, E F from 1919 until his death in 1940. E F Benson, besides being Mayor in the 1930s, made Rye (thinly disguised as Tillingham) famous with his comic Mapp and Lucia novels. Lamb House (National Trust) was also the home of Henry James from 1898, having moved from Point Hill in nearby Playden, also on the walk route. At Lamb House he wrote *The Wings of the Dove*, *The Ambassadors* and *The Golden Bowl* before returning to the United States in 1904.

*Opposite: Mermaid Street, Rye*

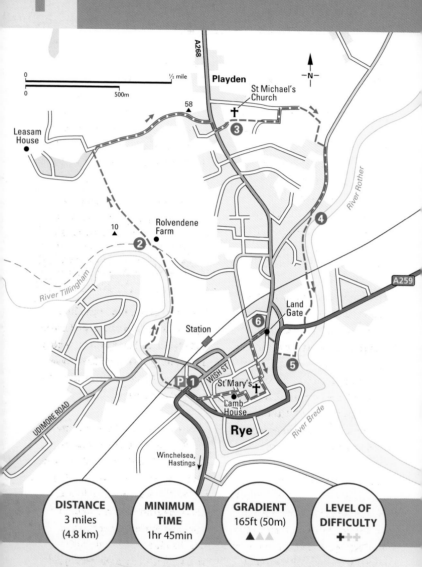

<table>
<thead>
<tr><th>DISTANCE</th><th>MINIMUM TIME</th><th>GRADIENT</th><th>LEVEL OF DIFFICULTY</th></tr>
</thead>
<tbody>
<tr><td>3 miles (4.8 km)</td><td>1hr 45min</td><td>165ft (50m) ▲▲▲</td><td>✚✚✚</td></tr>
</tbody>
</table>

**PATHS** Pavements and cobbles in Rye, then footpaths, mostly in pasture, some lanes, 3 stiles **LANDSCAPE** Fine historic townscape, river banks, sheep pasture and long views **SUGGESTED MAP** OS Explorer 125 Romney Marsh, Rye & Winchelsea **START/FINISH** Grid reference: TQ 917202 **DOG FRIENDLINESS** Dogs on lead in the sheep meadows along the River Tillingham and within the town of Rye **PARKING** Kettle of Fish pay car park by the roundabout where Winchelsea Road meets Strand Quay **PUBLIC TOILETS** Several in Rye

## WALK 1 DIRECTIONS

❶ From the car park turn right and just before the River Tillingham sluice go right at the footpath sign. Follow the river, crossing the railway line via gates and passing to the left of the windmill. Over Udimore Road climb a stile, cross a water-meadow and rejoin the river bank. Where the tarmac path veers right go left through a kissing gate to continue along the river bank, leaving it to bear right at a hedged drain towards a farm, Rolvendene Farm.

❷ Passing to its left, the path climbs out of the water-meadows alongside a fence to a bridle gate. Through a kissing gate continue uphill between fences, going right just before trees at the footpath sign along Leasham House's drive. Becoming a lane, follow this eastward to the A268, and turn right. Beyond the bus shelter turn left to St Michael's Church, Playden.

❸ Leave the far corner of the churchyard via a gate. Beyond a hedge, continue across a field to a footpath post. Turn left to a gate. Through this go right along a track which becomes a path. Through a gate admire the views over Romney Marshes and go right over a stile. Half right across the field descend to a gate. Through this go right to descend a tarmac lane.

❹ At Playden House turn right onto the pavement, going left at a footpath sign, opposite No 24. Through the kissing gate, bear right to walk along the bank of the River Rother. Before reaching the railway bridge the path leaves the river bank to pass behind houses, crosses the railway via two sets of gates on each side, and rejoins the river bank, soon crossing the A259.

> 🍴 **EATING AND DRINKING**
> The Strand Quay Café does all-day breakfasts as well as bacon rolls and sandwiches. There are numerous eating places and pubs in Rye, including the The Mermaid Inn.

❺ Past the play area go right. Turn right at the A259 to cross at pedestrian traffic lights. Go half right up a sloping path leading into the medieval town on its ridge. Facing you is the late 14th-century Land Gate.

❻ Go through Land Gate's arch and turn left into Tower Street. At Rope walk turn left up Conduit Hill. Cross the High Street into East Street, passing the Rye Castle Museum. At the house where the artist Paul Nash lived bear right, then left into Church square. Pass the Water House and visit St Mary's Church. Leave the churchyard at its north-west corner onto a narrow cobbled lane, West Street, and pass Lamb House. Turn left into Mermaid Street and descend towards the quays, passing The Mermaid Inn. Cross The Strand towards the 16th-century anchor in front of Rye Heritage Centre, and turn right to return to the car park.

# THE REMAINS OF AN ANCIENT CITY

Explore a 13th-century Cinque Port now more grass than house and which the sea has long deserted.

From the late 13th century until the mid-14th, Winchelsea thrived as an important port, specialising in the wine trade with English Gascony. Technically 'New Winchelsea', the town was planted on higher ground after the original Cinque Port of 'old' Winchelsea was washed away in 1287.

The town was laid out in 1283 and designed by an experienced builder of fortified planned towns, Itier Bochard. He laid out a grid of generous streets surrounding larger-than-normal plots for those times and also incorporated the old Anglo-Saxon village of Iham. Following Edward's promises of seven years occupation of a rent-free plot the town filled up rapidly.

## A Failed Port

Although initially successful, Winchelsea never filled its 39 'insulae' or groups of plots. Constant raids made the English Channel an extremely dangerous place in the Middle Ages, and Winchelsea suffered from French and Spanish raids during the Hundred Years War with much of the nave of the parish church of St Thomas destroyed and never rebuilt. The Black Death devastated the town and the walls were never completed, even after the King allowed the town to fortify a smaller area, and by the late 14th century rents were drastically reduced for the 387 tenements or houses.

Astonishingly, the town almost disappeared with only about 60 occupied houses by 1575 when the harbour had already silted up, the sea in retreat. The present town, or rather village, has dwellings only in 12 of the 39 'insulae' within the northern end of the town boundaries and the bulk of those are relatively modern. Fragments of the old town survive, for example a large number of stone cellars used by the merchants for storing imported wine, the magnificent early 14th-century choir of St Thomas' Church, the gable of one of the three medieval hospitals, three town gates, the remains of a Franciscan church and the old courthouse in the High Street. The two other parish churches, St Leonard and St Giles, have long disappeared. It is a great surprise to find the original south gate, New Gate, some 875yds (800m) south of the last house in Winchelsea and realise the town once stretched that far south.

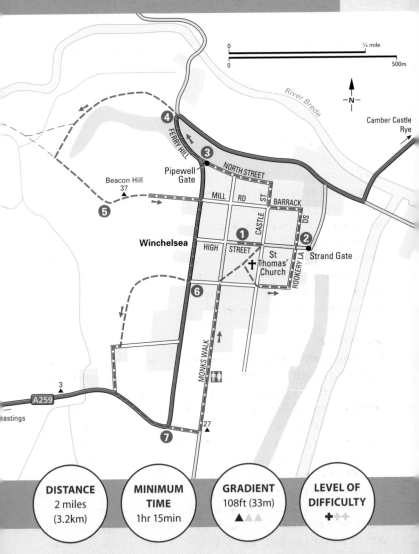

**DISTANCE**
2 miles
(3.2km)

**MINIMUM TIME**
1hr 15min

**GRADIENT**
108ft (33m)

**LEVEL OF DIFFICULTY**

**PATHS** Village pavements, some road verges and field paths, 1 stile
**LANDSCAPE** Ridge top town/village with wide views and sheep pasture
**SUGGESTED MAP** OS Explorer 124 Hastings & Bexhill or 125 Romney Marsh,
Rye & Winchelsea   **START/FINISH** Grid reference: TQ 905174
**DOG FRIENDLINESS** On lead in town and in sheep pasture to west of the town
**PARKING** Roadside parking in High Street near St Thomas Church at Winchelsea
**PUBLIC TOILETS** In Monks Walk, Winchelsea

## WALK 2 DIRECTIONS

**1** From the High Street, enter the churchyard to visit the church. Leave via the kissing gate in the south-east corner of the churchyard then along Rookery Lane (right of White Cottage). At the end turn left and pass a thatched stable with views to Dungeness.

**2** At the crossroads look right to 14th-century Strand Gate, but continue ahead along Barrack Square. At the end turn left into Mill Road and at the next crossroads turn right into Castle Street, passing Winchelsea Garden Shop. At the end go left into North Street to descend towards Pipewell Gate.

**3** Pass through the stone arch of Pipewell Gate, which was rebuilt around 1400 after the Spanish raid of 1380, descend Ferry Hill, now the A259, and at the hairpin bend go left over a stile beside a gate onto the 1066 Country Walk route.

**4** Now in the countryside, continue ahead past the Southern Water Treatment Works, over a footbridge and through a gate, then over two more footbridges and through a gate into a field. Go left alongside the old medieval town ditch and ramparts and at the footpath sign continue uphill, still beside the ditch with a view of Icklesham church tower ahead. Through a gate the path continues uphill, the valley increasingly far below to your right.

**5** Go left through a gate onto Beacon Hill, another fine viewpoint and the site of a windmill blown down in the 1987 storms and now with a Millennium Beacon. From the hill, head east to a gate and back towards the town, the path now Mill Lane. At the crossroads turn right along the pavement on the far side, passing the remains of Blackfriars Barn, actually the remains of a medieval house.

> **🍴 EATING AND DRINKING**
> The Little Shop in High Street, Winchelsea sells sandwiches and drinks. The New Inn does afternoon teas and home-cooked food.

**6** Go right through a kissing gate by a lamppost to cross the cricket field to a gate, continuing ahead to a footpath sign. Here go left now back alongside the town ramparts and ditch to descend towards the A259 amid sheep-cropped pastures. Go through a gate beside an old gasholder to continue ahead along a track. Reaching the main road turn left to walk along the grassy verge to climb back onto Winchelsea's ridge.

**7** At the crest cross the main road towards the narrow arch sign, passing on your right a stone gable wall, the remains of medieval St John's Hospital. At the junction turn left to follow the road alongside a stone wall, now in Monk's Walk, back to the church and the end of the walk.

# GREAT DIXTER AND ITS GLORIOUS GARDENS

Along the Sussex/Kent border, highlighting the skill and creativity of a famous architect and a gifted gardening writer.

Deep in the tranquil, rolling countryside of East Sussex, close to the Kent border, lies Great Dixter, one of the county's smaller and more intimate historic houses. It was built in the middle of the 15th century and later restored and enlarged by Sir Edwin Lutyens.

These days this Wealden hall-house is owned and cared for by Olivia Eller and was the home of her late uncle, Christopher Lloyd, the gardening writer, who died in 2006. It was Christopher's father, Nathaniel, who instructed Lutyens in 1910 to make major changes to Great Dixter and his main task was to clear the house of later alterations and, typically, the work was undertaken with great sensitivity.

One of Great Dixter's most striking features is the magnificent Great Hall, the largest surviving timber-framed hall in the country. The half-timbered and plastered front and the Tudor porch also catch the eye. The contents of Great Dixter date mainly from the 17th and 18th centuries and were collected over the years by Nathaniel Lloyd. The house also contains many examples of needlework, which were completed by his wife Daisy and their children.

## Impressive Gardens

The gardens are equally impressive. Christopher Lloyd spent many years working on this project, incorporating many medieval buildings, establishing natural ponds and designing yew topiary. The result is one of the most exciting, colourful and constantly changing gardens of modern times.

As with the house, plans were drawn up to improve the gardens, and here Lutyens was just as inventive. He often used tiles in a decorative though practical manner, to great effect. At Great Dixter he took a chicken house and transformed it into an open-sided loggia, supported by laminated tile pillars.

Beginning in Northiam, the walk heads round the edge of the village before reaching Great Dixter. Even out of season, when the place is closed, you gain a vivid impression of the house and its Sussex Weald setting. Passing directly in front of Great Dixter, the route then crosses rolling countryside to join the Sussex Border Path, following it all the way back to Northiam.

# Great Dixter

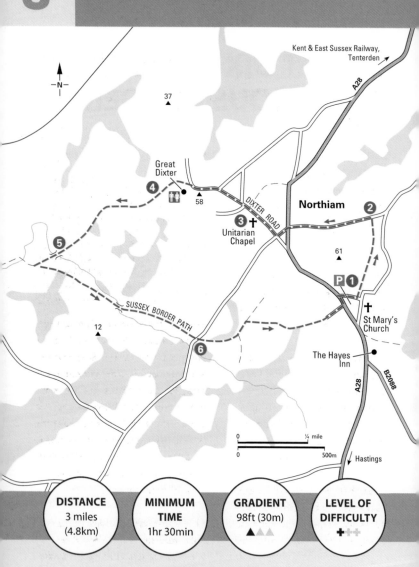

Kent & East Sussex Railway,
Tenterden

A28

—N—

37
▲

Great
Dixter

**4**  🚻

58
▲

DIXTER ROAD

**Northiam**

**2**

**5**

**3** ✝
Unitarian
Chapel

61
▲

🅿 **1**

SUSSEX BORDER PATH

12
▲

**6**

✝
St Mary's
Church

The Hayes
Inn

B2088

A28

0 ───────────── ¼ mile
0 ───────────── 500m

↙ Hastings

| **DISTANCE** | **MINIMUM TIME** | **GRADIENT** | **LEVEL OF DIFFICULTY** |
|:---:|:---:|:---:|:---:|
| 3 miles (4.8km) | 1hr 30min | 98ft (30m) ▲▲▲ | ✚ ✚✚ |

**PATHS** Field paths and quiet roads, 8 stiles
**LANDSCAPE** Undulating farmland and stretches of woodland
**SUGGESTED MAP** OS Explorer 125 Romney Marsh, Rye & Winchelsea
**START/FINISH** Grid reference: TQ 828245
**DOG FRIENDLINESS** Dog stiles near Great Dixter and on Sussex Border Path
**PARKING** Free car park on corner of Fullers Lane and A28, Northiam
**PUBLIC TOILETS** Great Dixter, seasonal opening

## WALK 3 DIRECTIONS

❶ Turn right out of the car park and along Fullers Lane towards St Mary's Church. Take the path on the left, signed to Goddens Gill, and keep to the right edge of the field. Go through a gate in the corner and look for an oasthouse on the right. Make for a path on the far side of the field and follow it between fences towards a thatched cottage. Go through a gate to the road.

❷ Turn left and head for the A28. Bear diagonally left across the A28 and follow Thyssel Lane signed 'Great Dixter'. Turn right at the crossroads, following Dixter Road.

❸ Pass the Unitarian Chapel and avoid the path on the right. Pass Higham Lane on the left, following signs for Great Dixter. Disregard a turning on the right (Dixter Lane) and go head, on a path between trees and hedges, parallel to the main drive to the house.

❹ Pass the toilets and head towards a cattle grid. Cross the stile just to the left of it and follow the path signed to Ewhurst. Follow the waymarks and

### 🍴 EATING AND DRINKING

The Hayes Inn at Northiam is open all day and serves bar food. Alternatively, Pat-a-cake Bakery has a tea room. When Great Dixter is open, you can buy soft drinks and basic prepacked snacks from the gift shop. There is also a picnic area.

keep the hedge on the left. Cross a stile in the field corner then head diagonally down the field slope to the next stile. Follow the path down the field slope.

### 🌿 IN THE AREA

Take a train ride on the Kent and East Sussex Railway. The railway opened in 1900 and ran from Robertsbridge to Headcorn, and was used mainly for taking farm produce to market, and for bringing in coal to drive machinery and for household fires. The coal yard at the station is still in use. The line closed to passengers in 1954 and to goods in 1961.

❺ Make for a footbridge then turn left to join the Sussex Border Path. The path skirts a field before disappearing left into woodland. Emerging from the trees, cut straight across the next field to two stiles and a footbridge. Keep the woodland left and look for a gap in the trees. Cross a stream to a stile and bear right. Follow the right edge of the field and keep on the Sussex Border Path until you reach the road.

❻ Cross the road to a drive. Bear left and follow the path to a stile. Pass alongside woodland then veer slightly away from the trees to a stile in the boundary. Cross it and go up the field slope. Take the first footpath on the right and follow it to a gap in the field corner. Cross a footbridge and continue along the right-hand edge of the field to join a drive. Bear left and follow it to the A28. Cross to return to the car park.

# A PERFECT CASTLE

Built in a time of devastating French raids on Sussex, Bodiam's 14th-century towers exude military strength.

### 'For the Resistence of our Enemies'

No medieval lord was allowed to build a castle or even put a battlement on his manor house without obtaining a formal Licence to Crenellate from the king. In 1385 the ill-fated king, Richard II, granted Bodiam manor's owner, Sir Edward Dalyngrigge, licence to crenellate his house. To put this in context, French and Spanish raids had recently devastated Rye and Winchelsea (Walks 1 ands 2) and Sir Edward's case was strengthened by his claim that Bodiam could defend the Rother Valley as an outpost of Rye, and to a lesser extent of Winchelsea, from the ravages of the French. Indeed the river was then fully navigable for quite large vessels up to Bodiam Bridge.

The castle was completed quickly for Sir Edward whose rise in royal favour continued, soon becoming Keeper of the Tower (of London). When he died in 1295 it was complete, set within elaborate water defences. The moat, or rather a large lake, some 500ft (152m) by 350ft (107m) is fed by water diverted from the Rother. The castle plan is a hollow rectangle, with drum towers at the corners and further towers and gatehouses in the centre of each side.

In Tudor times the complex, drawbridges and islands were replaced with a causeway. As originally built, the defences had no less than three drawbridges leading to the main entrance across the moat and two to defend the now vanished postern or rear entrance. There were 'arrow slits' designed for small cannon while inside comfort was attended to with over 30 fireplaces, 28 lavatories or 'privies' and generous-sized windows to domestic apartments.

There may well have been more fireplaces as the interior was gutted after a depressingly brief siege by Parliamentary forces in 1643 during the Civil War, fortunately leaving the outer walls more or less intact. Falling into serious disrepair it was finally taken in hand by Lord Curzon in 1919, who restored it with care and later passed it to the National Trust.

Now one of the National Trust's most popular buildings, it is open every day from mid-February until the end of October and on fewer days per week in winter. There is a very good café, its name, Wharf Tea Room, recalling the river trade along the Rother, as well as parking and toilets.

*Opposite: The elaborate defences of Bodiam Castle*

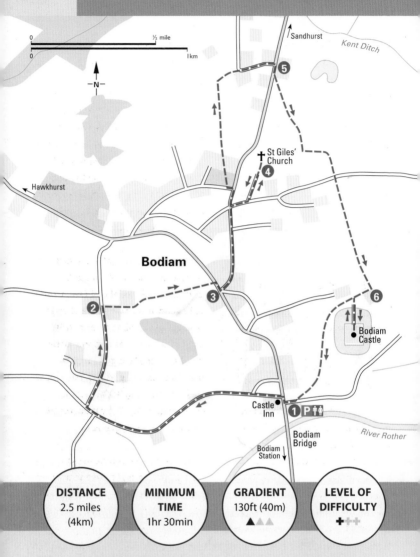

½ mile

0

0                    1km

—N—

↑ Sandhurst

Kent Ditch

**5**

✝ St Giles'
Church
**4**

← Hawkhurst

**Bodiam**

**2**

**3**

**6**

● Bodiam
Castle

Castle
Inn
**1** P ♿

Bodiam
Bridge

Bodiam
Station ↓

River Rother

| DISTANCE | MINIMUM TIME | GRADIENT | LEVEL OF DIFFICULTY |
|---|---|---|---|
| 2.5 miles (4km) | 1hr 30min | 130ft (40m) ▲▲▲ | ✚✚✚ |

**PATHS** A stretch of road, lanes and field paths, 6 stiles
**LANDSCAPE** River valley and gentle hills  **SUGGESTED MAP** OS Explorer
136 High Weald  **START/FINISH** Grid reference: TQ 784253
**DOG FRIENDLINESS** On a lead by Knowle Hill Kennels (horses in the fields),
and north-west of Bodiam church where there are sheep
**PARKING** National Trust car park at Bodiam Castle (£2 or free for NT members)
**PUBLIC TOILETS** Bodiam Castle car park

Bodiam Walk
# 4

## WALK 4 DIRECTIONS

**1** Leave the car park and turn right, then left by the Castle Inn to walk left of the small village green along a lane marked 'Private Road' with views south towards Bodiam station on the Kent and East Sussex Railway, if lucky with a steam-hauled train simmering gently. Continue past The Old Cricket Pavilion, now a cottage. At a track T-junction you turn right uphill, the lane climbing to pass well to the right of some converted oasthouses.

> **🍴 EATING AND DRINKING**
> The Wharf Tea Room at Bodiam is excellent and in good weather outside tables have good views over the Rother Valley. Near the entrance is the Castle Inn, which does tasty bar food and snacks.

**2** At the crest and opposite a large modern farm building go right, then to a hand gate between two pairs of five-barred field gates. Descend to the left of cottages to a guidepost. Skirt a red-brick farm building, passing a great number of dachshunds in the kennel runs, and then head left towards a stile. Over the stile go right alongside a hedge and over a stile onto the road.

**3** Cross the road to the lane going to the right of the Old School House, formerly a Victorian schoolmaster's house with the modern school behind it. Walk along the pavement northwards and at the sign for St Giles' Church follow the path and go through the lychgate into the churchyard.

**4** Retrace your steps to the road. In Levetts Lane bear right through the woods to the footpath between Nos 35 and 34. Over a stile descend into the valley through pasture. Through a field gate, cross to another. Over this one head right to another field gate onto a lane, continue ahead past Bramble Cottage to a road junction.

**5** At the lane turn right and shortly bear half left into a field to climb towards an oak tree ahead. Over a stile go left and over another one, shortly bearing right to climb another stile. Cross a track to a tree gap and to the left of a double field gate continue ahead alongside a post and wire fence, the battlements of Bodiam Castle ahead in its valley. The path descends between vineyards to a stile.

**6** Across the stile you are in the grounds of Bodiam Castle. Follow the path to visit the castle, afterwards skirt it to the right to return to the car park.

> **🦢 ON THE WALK**
> St Giles' pretty parish church with its sweeping tiled roofs is well away from Bodiam's village centre. It is set in a churchyard surrounded by trees and overlooks a deep-cut sunken lane where the road drops into the valley of the Kent Ditch, a minor tributary of the Rother.

# A DROWNED VALLEY

Bewl Water, created in the 1970s, has naturalised superbly and now attracts innumerable wildfowl.

Walking is only one of the many activities taking place around Bewl Water, the 770-acre (311ha) reservoir formed by damming the upper reaches of the River Bewl just before it flows into Kent. Work started in 1973 and the reservoir, which was completed in 1975, was given a head start by receiving over 7 million gallons (31 million litres) of water to supplement the less fruitful River Bewl. Most of this extra water came from the River Medway, which is regularly used to top up Bewl Water. Flooding these valleys has, it is claimed, created the largest freshwater lake (artificial or natural) in England.

The northern shores are followed by the Sussex Border Path, but there are over 17 miles (27km) of foreshore altogether. The lake has rapidly become one of the country's finest fly fishing venues, both from boats and from the shore. There is a very successful sailing club and the visitor centre has a thriving restaurant, the Food Court Restaurant. Bikes and rowing boats can be hired and there is a waymarked 'Round Bewl' cycle trail. Canoeing, windsurfing and boat trips add to the range of activities. You can even hire the visitor centre for weddings, conferences and other events.

## Coppice Restoration

For the walker, however, you can soon get away from the activities in the visitor centre and car park areas. This route follows the northern side of the lake where, beside numerous birds and other wildlife, there are areas of traditional sweet chestnut coppicing being revived after years of disuse.

On the route, the coppice woods around the Hook Farm area are currently being restored with tall oaks retained as timber trees or 'standards'. To create coppice trees a young chestnut (or hazel or ash, for example) tree would be cut to the ground or 'coppiced' and the re-growth cut on a regular cycle for use in furniture making, fencing (chestnut paling), etc. In this area, of course, coppicing also fed the Sussex and Kentish Weald's medieval and Tudor iron industry whose appetite for fuel-timber and charcoal was very considerable. Indeed the Weald was only overtaken as England's major iron producing areas in the 18th century.

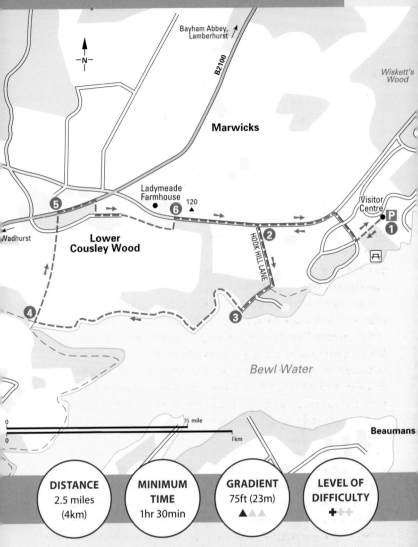

Wiskett's Wood

B2100

**Marwicks**

Ladymeade Farmhouse ● 120 ▲ ⑥

⑤

Hadhurst ←

**Lower Cousley Wood**

Visitor Centre ⓟ ①

HOOK HILL LANE

②

④

③

*Bewl Water*

Beaumans

0 ——— ½ mile
0 ——— 1 km

| DISTANCE | MINIMUM TIME | GRADIENT | LEVEL OF DIFFICULTY |
|---|---|---|---|
| 2.5 miles (4km) | 1hr 30min | 75ft (23m) ▲△△ | ✚✚✚ |

**PATHS** A stretch of lanes, lakeside and field paths, 10 stiles

**LANDSCAPE** Lakeside, woods and fields

**SUGGESTED MAP** OS Explorer 136 High Weald Royal Tunbridge Wells

**START/FINISH** Grid reference: TQ 675337

**DOG FRIENDLINESS** On a lead in fields outside Bewl Water's perimeter

**PARKING** Bewl Water Visitor Centre car park (parking fee)

**PUBLIC TOILETS** In the visitor centre

## WALK 5 DIRECTIONS

**❶** From the car park north of the visitor centre follow the exit signs (for vehicles) and 'Round Bewl' cycle markers posts, pass the horsebox parking area and the entrance to Bewl Valley Sailing Club. At the road exit go left past a barrier onto a tree-shaded vehicle-free sunken lane and follow this to the junction with Hook Hill Lane.

**❷** Turn left into Hook Hill Lane which descends to a bend and bears right to continue downhill amid restored sweet chestnut coppiced woodland, soon passing a footpath sign to Bramble Bay. Go through a gate to enter Bewl Water's perimeter and continue towards the lake's side.

> **🍴 EATING AND DRINKING**
>
> The Food Court Restaurant recently refurbished and in the visitor's centre is open from 10am until 5pm virtually all year round, unless the building has been hired for a wedding or other function.

**❸** Go right and follow the bridleway, which runs mostly away from the lake amid trees. Emerging from the trees the path continues with views of the lake. At the end of the inlet and just before the lakeside path disappears into woodland go right to a stile, 'Lower Cousley Wood' on the footpath sign.

**❹** Over the stile go half right across pasture to climb to the next stile. Head across the next field to guidepost, then continue to field corner and over a stile. Soon go through a kissing gate, cross a gravel drive, through a woodland belt and out onto a road via a gate.

**❺** Go right along the lane verge and then right again down an entrance drive by a tall pine. Follow the gravelled drive to 'The Oasts' and pass to the left of its garage and through the garden. Continue ahead on the footpath along a grassy track to a stile. Continue ahead, crossing two stiles, then two more on either side of a track. Continue ahead to right of a brick outbuilding to a stile, then through gardens via a gate and another stile. Out of the last garden go left to another stile at the road.

**❻** Over this stile go right onto a lane and follow this back, continuing ahead at the junction with Hook Hill Lane and back to the car park at Bewl Water.

> **🐾 ON THE WALK**
>
> Walking beside Bewl Water you should see great crested grebe and heron competing with the anglers and numerous geese, some passing through in their spring and autumn migrations. There are always many other species of wildfowl including tufted ducks, teal, pochard, moorhens and widgeon.

# A TOWN AND ITS ABBEY

Robertsbridge is a town full of history and historic buildings set in rolling hop-growing Sussex countryside.

When founded in 1176 Robertsbridge Abbey, the only Cistercian abbey in Sussex, was situated in the High Street near today's George Inn and the war memorial. It was an important abbey visited by kings, such as Henry III and Edward II. Buried there were notables such as Sir Edward Dalyngrigge and his wife, the builder of Bodiam Castle (Walk 4) and Sir John Pelham who helped capture John II, the king of France, at the Battle of Poitiers in 1356.

Of the abbey remains, the present house was the abbot's lodging, although much altered and largely screened from public view it contains much 13th-century work including the abbot's great hall roof. What you can see from the lane is a high, stone wall which was part of the monk's Refectory or dining hall. Further east is more abbey walling but unseen from the lane. After Henry VIII dissolved the abbey in 1538, much was left standing and survived until the late 18th century when it was used it as a source of building stone. Indeed if you look carefully in the town, stones and timber from it can be seen, including a carved roof boss in the church rooms you pass in Fair lane.

### The Kentish Hop and the Oasthouse

In the autumn, when the hops from the fields around Robertsbridge have been harvested, you may be lucky enough to see an oasthouse in action and catch the scent of drying hops on the air. Oasthouses have characteristic conical or tapering pyramidal roofs with a vent cowl at the top. Below is a floor laid with narrow gaps between the boards and joists that are usually covered by sacking. This floor is at first floor level and below is the fire, sometimes, as at Redlands Farm on this route, outside the oasthouse with fans to direct the hot air into the building (less of a fire risk). The hops are spread out to dry, the hot air from fires below the drying floors being drawn through the thin floor by the updraught provided by the oast 'chimney'.

Hops, of course, were crucial to the brewing industry, but nowadays locally grown ones tend to be used at the premium end of the market, imported hops having largely taken over in large-scale beer brewing, but it is good to know some is still grown and processed around Robertsbridge.

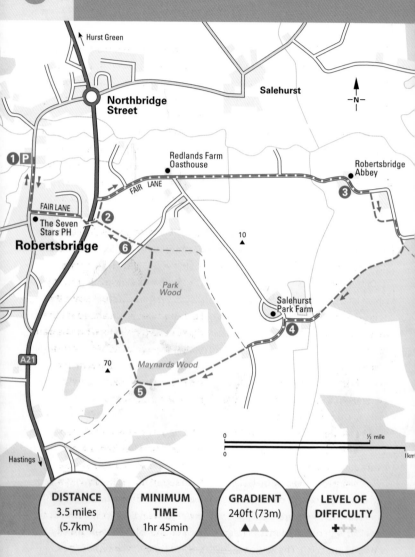

Hurst Green

—N—

Salehurst

Northbridge
Street

**1** P

Redlands Farm
Oasthouse

Robertsbridge
Abbey

**3**

FAIR LANE

FAIR LANE

**2**

The Seven
Stars PH

**Robertsbridge**

**6**

10 ▲

Park
Wood

Salehurst
Park Farm

**4**

A21

70 ▲

Maynards Wood

**5**

Hastings

0 ½ mile
0 1km

| **DISTANCE**<br>3.5 miles<br>(5.7km) | **MINIMUM<br>TIME**<br>1hr 45min | **GRADIENT**<br>240ft (73m)<br>▲▲▲ | **LEVEL OF<br>DIFFICULTY**<br>✛✛✛ |
|---|---|---|---|

**PATHS** Some lanes and farm tracks, woodland and field paths, 4 stiles
**LANDSCAPE** Rolling Sussex countryside, woods and an historic town
**SUGGESTED MAP** OS Explorer 124 Hastings & Bexhill
**START/FINISH** Grid reference: TQ 737238 **DOG FRIENDLINESS** On a lead in the
fields that have cattle and sheep grazing **PARKING** Robertsbridge Cricket Club
Car Park, The Clappers, at north end of the old town (also a free public car park)
**PUBLIC TOILETS** At car park awaiting repair and re-opening shortly

## WALK 6 DIRECTIONS

❶ From the car park turn right and then walk towards the town centre, turning left into Fair Lane, just before The Seven Stars, a fine 15th-century timber-framed building serving the excellent Harveys beers from Lewes. Continue ahead and cross over the A21 on a footbridge.

❷ Across the bridge bear left to descend and rejoin Fair Lane, a lane bisected by the bypass. Continue along the lane and pass Redlands, a farm that still has a working oasthouse that dries hops from its own fields. Continue along the lane which bears right to pass Robertsbridge Abbey's somewhat scanty remains.

❸ Continue along the lane until a footpath sign just before gates and farm sheds; go right and continue between fences. At the end go right onto a concrete track which you follow until it bears left. Here continue ahead on a track, going right before reaching some gates to follow a footpath within the edge of woodland. Through a field gate descend in sheep pasture to another field gate. Continue ahead on a track that curves gently right to a T-junction.

❹ At the T-junction, near Salehurst Park Farm, go left onto a track that climbs to the right, enjoying more good views, including oast towers, hop fields and Salehurst church spire. Continue ahead at a crossway, now on a footpath rather than a track. Through a field gate continue ahead towards the crest where the path bears right into the edge of Maynards Wood.

❺ Still within Maynards Wood, bear right at a footpath sign and continue along a track, then go over a stile. Continue ahead alongside a recently planted hedge in pasture. Leave the field via a stile and after ten paces go right into Park Wood to follow the main path as it gently descends. Eventually take a left fork (the main path) and emerge from the woods at a stile beside a sewage works.

❻ Descend into the valley bottom between chain link fences, then continue ahead to cross an arable field alongside a hedge. At the field corner go left onto a footpath within the edge of a copse. This path curves right to rejoin the footbridge over the A21. Across this continue back down Fair Lane and turn right back to the car park.

---

🍴 **EATING AND DRINKING**

There are plenty of watering holes in Robertsbridge and The Seven Stars is on the route. Besides serving Harveys real ales it also does good home-cooked food, as does The George Inn further south in the High Street. There are also cafés and restaurants in this delightful and historic main street.

# TOWERING ROMAN WALLS

Once with the sea on three sides, Pevensey has spectacular remains of a Roman fortress and Norman castle.

Pevensey Castle whose massive, craggy flint walls dominate this small town was not built as a castle but as a Roman fortress around AD340 as part of Britannia's defences against marauding Saxons and named Anderida. The land was very different then with the sea lapping its south walls, a deep harbour to its east and north and marshes beyond.

After the Romans left, the local Britons were massacred in AD491 by a Saxon army led by the fearsome Aella and Cissa. Pevensey reappeared in history when the Normans conquered England in 1066, landing here before marching east to Hastings. Granted to Robert of Mortain, William the Conqueror's half brother, the Roman fortress was turned into a fully fledged medieval castle, utilising the Roman walls as the outer bailey. The south-east corner was walled and moated to form an inner bailey with a tall keep.

The castle had an active history during the Middle Ages but fell into disuse in Tudor times. It had a brief military revival in the Second World War as a fully garrisoned observation and command post. It is now an English Heritage site and the scale of the surviving Roman walls and towers is remarkable, with two gateways having survived largely intact.

Outside the west gate the village of Westham is mentioned in the Domesday Book of 1087 and looks more like a small market town.

## The Pevensey Levels

Leaving Pevensey, the route takes you out onto the Levels, as these vast flat areas of rich pasture land are called. In Roman times the marshes and fens were of use to neither man nor beast, the new Norman landowners, including the lords of Pevensey and the Abbot of Battle, set about converting the salt marshes into useful land, building sea dykes and drains, many of which survive. Salt making was also of importance on the salt marshes.

However, the sea fought back in the later Middle Ages and much of the Levels were abandoned to the sea's fury. In calmer times, Pevensey was marooned inland, its port long gone, and the Levels were eventually reclaimed again.

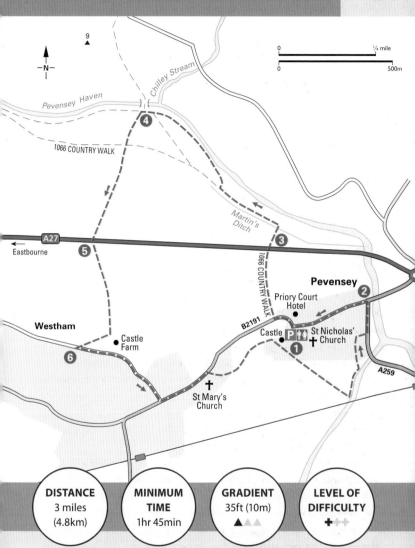

9 ▲

−N−

Chilley Stream

Pevensey Haven

0   ¼ mile
0   500m

④

1066 COUNTRY WALK

Martin's Ditch

**A27**

← Eastbourne

⑤

③

②

**Pevensey**

Priory Court Hotel

1066 COUNTRY WALK

B2191

Castle P ⑤ St Nicholas' + Church

①

**Westham**

● Castle Farm

⑥

✝ St Mary's Church

A259

| DISTANCE | MINIMUM TIME | GRADIENT | LEVEL OF DIFFICULTY |
|----------|--------------|----------|---------------------|
| 3 miles (4.8km) | 1hr 45min | 35ft (10m) ▲△△ | ✚✚✚ |

**PATHS** Some lanes and farm tracks, woodland and field paths, 5 stiles
**LANDSCAPE** A low ridge with Pevensey and Westham above the Levels, drained former marshes, now rich sheep pasture  **SUGGESTED MAP** OS Explorer 124 Hastings & Bexhill  **START/FINISH** Grid reference: TQ 646047
**DOG FRIENDLINESS** On a lead in the Levels where sheep graze
**PARKING** Pevensey Castle Car Park (outside the castle's east gate)
**PUBLIC TOILETS** In the car park

## WALK 7 DIRECTIONS

**1** From the far end of the car park leave via a gate, cross to a footbridge and turn left. Now in Anderida Park continue alongside a hedge to the end and go left over a footbridge to continue by sports pitches, the river to your right. At a car park in Pevensey Recreation Ground bear right to the road. Turn left to traffic lights.

**2** Turn left to walk along Pevensey's High Street towards the castle, diverting south to visit the church. Returning to High Street continue past the castle entrance and bear right into Castle Road, passing the Priory Court Hotel. Leave the road going right on a footpath, signed '1066 Country Walk'. Follow this to the A27, crossing it with care via a bridle gate each side.

> ### 🍴 EATING AND DRINKING
> By the car park is the Castle Cottage Tea Room and opposite is The Royal Oak and Castle Inn. Further east, in the High Street is The Smugglers and in Westham, The Heron. All do food.

**3** Continue along a fenced path that bears left beyond Martin's Ditch. Continue alongside this to a bridle gate. Through this bear right to walk along the river bank, the Pevensey Haven, as far as a footbridge.

**4** Don't cross the footbridge, but turn left and head south to a stile. Over this, go through a field gate to keep ahead, now in sheep pasture. Pass between gateposts and over a causeway across a drainage ditch. Bear quarter left to a footpath post, cross a drain and continue to cross the A27 via a stile.

**5** Descending to a stile, cross a footbridge with a stile at each end and head across pasture to a footbridge and stile. Over this aim slightly to the right of an electricity pole, now ascending back onto the ridge, shortly seeing Westham's church tower. At the crest descend to a gate and just before the farm buildings of Castle Farm bear quarter right and head for a stile.

**6** Over this go left and follow the lane past the entrance to Castle Farm. Shortly pass a pond and Westham Village Hall. At the main street turn left to walk through Westham to St Mary's Church. Continue past a small green with a Georgian cannon and enter Pevensey Castle's grounds via a gate and then the Norman west gate. Visit the Norman castle keep and leave via the east gate back to the car park.

> ### 🕑 IN THE AREA
> In nearby Eastbourne visit the Redoubt Fortress and Military Museum on Royal Parade east of the town centre. Much larger than the famous chain of contemporary Martello towers, the fortress had 24 massive cannon. Nowadays it is a superb museum, the Military Museum of Sussex.

# NEOLITHIC DOWNLANDS

A bracing downland walk, to a partly Anglo-Saxon church and New Stone Age earthworks.

On Combe Hill we come into contact with our ancient forebears, for around the crest of the hill a neolithic or New Stone Age camp was built on a causeway surrounded by two concentric ditches. These camps date back to 3000BC and there are four known in Sussex, The Trundle above Chichester being the most famous. No one knows for sure what they were used for but informed suggestions include tribal gatherings, corralling animals, protection in times of danger or for the predecessors of markets and fairs. Also on the hill are the humps of tumuli or burial mounds and ancient field systems.

This area is rich in archaeology and, together with a further 4,000 acres (1,620ha), was purchased in 1929 by the enlightened corporation of Eastbourne to conserve the downs west of Eastbourne for its citizens.

St Andrew's Church in Jevington would have more Anglo-Saxon evidence had the 1873 restoration been less drastic. Notwithstanding this, the tower is recognisably Anglo-Saxon and at least the ancient colonettes in the modern belfry openings are genuine ones reused.

The nave is also partly 11th century but the most well-known feature is the Jevington Slab, also Anglo-Saxon or rather Anglo-Scandinavian, so probably early 11th century when England was rules by Danish kings. It is a figure of Christ in a loincloth and by His feet writhing foliage carved in the Scandinavian 'Urnes' style. How it got here is unknown but it was found in the tower in 1785 and is now mounted on the north wall.

## A Smugglers' Tale

Jevington and surrounding areas were hotbeds of smuggling in the 18th century. Indeed Alfriston on the Cuckmere River to the west now trades on its smuggling past. In the late 18th century James Pettit led the smugglers of Jevington. Locally known as 'Jevington Jigg', he was the landlord of the local inn, now The Eight Bells and on the walk route. One of his escapes from the excise officers was made in women's clothing but he was eventually convicted for horse stealing and transported in 1799 to the recently established convict settlement of Botany Bay in Australia.

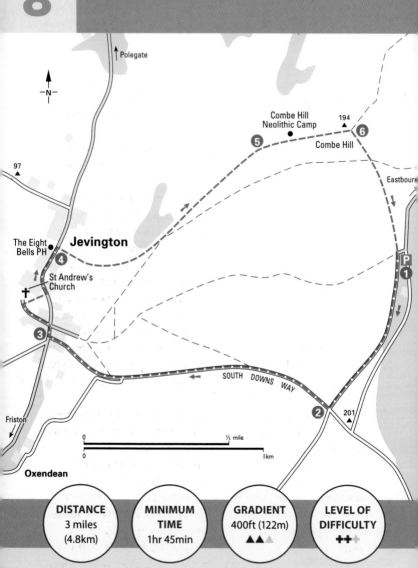

Jevington

↑ Polegate

—N—

Combe Hill
Neolithic Camp

194 ▲

**5**

**6**

Combe Hill

97 ▲

Eastbour

The Eight
Bells PH •

**Jevington**

**4**

✝ St Andrew's
Church

**3**

SOUTH   DOWNS   WAY

Friston

**2**

201 ▲

0                    ½ mile

0                                    1km

**Oxendean**

| DISTANCE | MINIMUM TIME | GRADIENT | LEVEL OF DIFFICULTY |
|---|---|---|---|
| 3 miles (4.8km) | 1hr 45min | 400ft (122m) ▲▲▲ | ++✚ |

**PATHS** Downland tracks and field paths with a short stretch of lane in Jevington village, 2 stiles **LANDSCAPE** Up high on the South Downs, mainly grassland with long views and deep-cut combes **SUGGESTED MAP** OS Explorer 123 Eastbourne & Beachy Head **START/FINISH** Grid reference: TQ 579017
**DOG FRIENDLINESS** On a lead towards Combe Hill on the northern leg of the route amid grazing sheep **PARKING** Butts Brow pay-and-display car park, accessed via Willingdon off the A22 **PUBLIC TOILETS** None on route

## WALK 8 DIRECTIONS

❶ From the car park car head south towards Beachy Head as indicated on The stone sign block and guidepost. the deep combe of Willingdon Bottom is away to your right, then Eastbourne to your left as you steadily ascend and looking right you can see Jevington church and the heavily wooded slopes behind it.

❷ At the crest, now at about 640ft (195m) above sea level, you reach a footpath junction with the South Downs Way long distance footpath. Bear right onto the Way and descend towards Jevington, the flat-bottomed dry valley of Harewick Bottom to your left and sheep grazing beyond the path's post and wire fences. Nearing Jevington the path becomes an old hill pasture access lane.

❸ Reaching Jevington turn right onto the village street. Pass the Jevington Tea Garden and, opposite The Hungry Monk restaurant, go left into Church Lane. At the churchyard leave the South Downs Way to pass to the right of the church, then continue alongside the high flint boundary wall to Jevington Place. Leaving the churchyard via a rotating timber gate, the path bears left alongside the village road to The Eight Bells pub.

❹ Opposite the pub go right onto the footpath up steps. Shortly the path continues ahead climbing steadily between post and wire fences to a kissing gate. Through this go half left to the next kissing gate through a field with ponies to another kissing gate, then continue half left to a guidepost, now on sheep cropped downland. Continue ahead to next guidepost and, forking left, ascend to a stile with long views north towards the Weald.

❺ Over the stile continue ahead to a gap in the scrub and over another stile pass between the gorse and thorn, beyond it continuing ahead to a summit littered with tumuli.

❻ The summit is Combe Hill, ringed by a neolithic causeway camp, its ramparts relatively clear. To the north the escarpment descends very steeply into The Combe and you can see Polegate Windmill rising out of its suburban surroundings. At the guidepost beyond the 633ft(193m) summit bear right to descend, the path bearing gently right, then ahead and back to the car park.

# ARLINGTON'S LAKESIDE TRAIL

Combine this delightful walk with a little birding as you explore the banks of a reservoir by the Cuckmere River.

It was in 1971 that Arlington's rural landscape changed irrevocably in both character and identity. A vital new reservoir was opened, supplying water to the nearby communities of Eastbourne, Hailsham, Polegate and Heathfield.

The 120-acre (49ha) reservoir was formed by cutting off a meander in the Cuckmere River and it's now an established site for wintering wildfowl, as well as home to a successful rainbow trout fishery. Besides the trout, bream, perch, roach and eels make up Arlington's underwater population. Fly fishing is a popular activity here and the lake draws anglers from all over Sussex.

The local nature reserve was originally planted with more than 30,000 native trees, including oak, birch, wild cherry, hazel and hawthorn. The grassland areas along the shoreline are left uncut intentionally to enable many kinds of moth and butterfly to thrive in their natural habitats. Orchids grow here too.

## Birding

Arlington Reservoir, a designated Site of Special Scientific Interest (SSSI), is a favourite haunt of many birds on spring and autumn migrations and up to 10,000 wildfowl spend their winter here, including large numbers of mallard and wigeon. The shoveler duck is also a frequent visitor and most common as a bird of passage. Great crested grebes, Canada geese and nightingales are also known to inhabit the reservoir area, making Arlington a popular destination for ornithologists. See if you can spot the blue flash of a kingfisher on the water, its colouring so distinctive it would be hard to confuse it with any other bird. It's also known for its piercing whistles as it swoops low over the water. The reservoir and its environs are also home to fallow deer and foxes, so keep a sharp look-out as you walk around the lake.

The walk begins in the main car park by the reservoir, though initially views of the lake are obscured by undergrowth and a curtain of trees. Be patient. After visiting the village of Arlington, where there is a welcome pub, the return leg is directly beside the water, providing a constantly changing scenic backdrop to round off the walk.

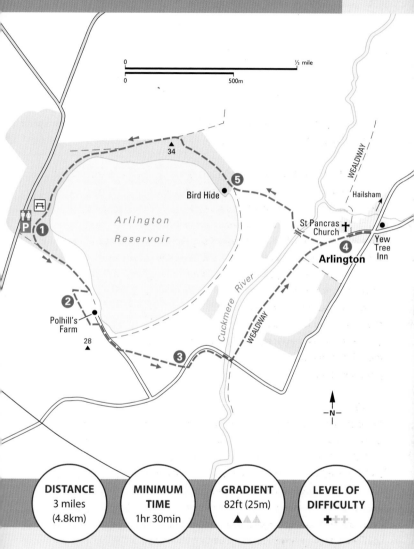

WEALDWAY

Hailsham

Bird Hide

St Pancras Church

Yew Tree Inn

**Arlington**

Arlington Reservoir

Cuckmere River

WEALDWAY

Polhill's Farm

28

34

0        ½ mile
0              500m

—N—

| **DISTANCE** | **MINIMUM TIME** | **GRADIENT** | **LEVEL OF DIFFICULTY** |
|---|---|---|---|
| 3 miles (4.8km) | 1hr 30min | 82ft (25m) ▲▲▲ | ✚✚✚ |

**PATHS** Field paths and trail, some brief road walking, 13 stiles
**LANDSCAPE** Level lakeside terrain and gentle farmland
**SUGGESTED MAP** OS Explorer 123 Eastbourne & Beachy Head
**START/FINISH** Grid reference: TQ 528074
**DOG FRIENDLINESS** Mostly on lead, as requested by signs on route
**PARKING** Fee-paying car park at Arlington Reservoir
**PUBLIC TOILETS** At car park

## WALK 9 DIRECTIONS

❶ From the car park walk towards the information boards and then turn right to join the waymarked bridleway. Cut through the trees to a tarmac lane and look for a bridleway sign. Follow the lane and soon the reservoir edges into view again. On reaching a gate signed 'No entry – farm access only' bear right and follow the bridleway and footpath signs.

❷ Skirt the buildings of Polhill's Farm and return to walk along the tarmac lane. Turn right and walk along to a kissing gate and a 'circular walk' sign. Ignore the gate and keep on the lane. Continue for about 100yds (91m) and then branch left over a stile into a field. Swing half right and look for a second stile to the right of an overgrown pond. Cross a third stile and go across a pasture to a fourth stile.

❸ Cross the road and follow the path parallel with the road. Rejoin the road, cross the Cuckmere River and then bear left to join the Wealdway, following the sign for Arlington. Walk along the drive and when it curves to the right, by some houses, veer left over a stile. The spire of Arlington church can be seen now. Continue ahead when you reach the right-hand fence corner, following the waymark. Cross several stiles and a footbridge. Keep to the right of the church, cross another stile and pass the Old School on the right.

❹ Walk along the lane to the Yew Tree Inn, then retrace your steps to the church and cross over the field to the footbridge. Turn right immediately beyond it to a stile in the field corner. Cross the pasture to the obvious footbridge and continue to cross over a plank bridge, then head across the field towards a line of trees, following the vague outline of a path. The reservoir's embankment is clearly defined on the left, as you begin a gentle ascent.

❺ Cross a stile by a galvanised gate and go through a kissing gate on the immediate right. Follow the path alongside the lake and pass a bird hide on the left. Turn left further on and keep to the bridleway as it reveals glimpses of the lake through the trees. Veer left at the fork and then follow the path alongside the reservoir back to the car park.

---

### ⑪ EATING AND DRINKING
Arlington Reservoir has a picnic site by the car park where you can relax before or after the walk. The Yew Tree Inn at Arlington has a children's play area, beer garden and a choice of home-cooked dishes. Lunch and dinner are served every day and there is a choice of real ales. Near by is the Old Oak Inn, originally the village almshouse and dating from 1733. The likes of Newhaven cod in batter, curry and steak-and-kidney pudding feature on the menu.

# THE SNAKE RIVER AND THE SEVEN SISTERS

Follow a breezy trail beside the Cuckmere River as it winds in erratic fashion towards the sea.

One of the few remaining undeveloped river mouths in the south-east, is the gap or cove known as Cuckmere Haven. It is one of the south coast's best-known and most popular beauty spots and was regularly used by smugglers in the 18th century to bring ashore their cargoes of brandy and lace. The scene has changed very little in the intervening years with the eternal surge of waves breaking on the isolated shore.

## Seven Sisters Country Park

The focal point of the lower valley is the Seven Sisters Country Park, an amenity area of 692 acres (280ha) developed by East Sussex County Council. The site is a perfect location for a country park and has been imaginatively planned to blend with the coastal beauty. There are artificial lakes and park trails, and an old Sussex barn near by has been converted to provide a visitor centre which includes many interesting exhibits and displays.

Wildlife plays a key role within the park's boundaries, while the flowers and insects found here are at their best in early to mid-summer, while spring and autumn are a good time for a close-up view of migrant birds.

Early migrant wheatears are sometimes spotted in the vicinity of the river mouth from late February onwards and are followed later in the season by martins, swallows, whinchats and warblers. Keep a careful eye out for whitethroats, terns and waders too. The lakes and lagoons tend to attract waders such as curlews, sandpipers and little stints. Grey phalaropes have also been seen in the park, usually after severe autumn storms.

The walk explores this very special part of the Cuckmere Valley and begins by heading for the beach. As you make your way there, you might wonder why the river meanders the way it does. The meltwaters of the last ice age shaped this landscape, and over the centuries rising sea levels and a freshwater peat swamp influenced the river's route to the Channel. Around the start of the 19th century, the sea rose to today's level and a straight cut with raised banks, devised in 1846, shortened the Cuckmere's journey to the sea. This unnatural waterway controls the river and helps prevent flooding.

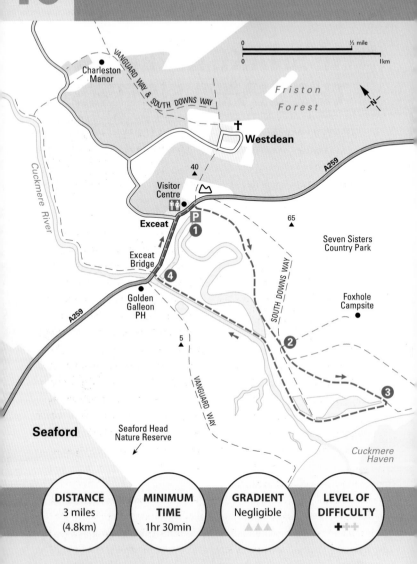

DISTANCE
3 miles
(4.8km)

MINIMUM
TIME
1hr 30min

GRADIENT
Negligible
▲▲▲

LEVEL OF
DIFFICULTY
✚╬╬

**PATHS** Grassy trails and well-used paths, mostly beside the Cuckmere
or canalised branch of river **LANDSCAPE** Exposed and isolated valley
and river mouth **SUGGESTED MAP** OS Explorer 123 Eastbourne & Beachy Head
**START/FINISH** Grid reference: TV 518995 **DOG FRIENDLINESS** Under close
control within Seven Sisters Country Park. On lead during lambing season and
near A259 **PARKING** Fee-paying car park at Seven Sisters Country Park
**PUBLIC TOILETS** Opposite car park, by visitor centre

## WALK 10 DIRECTIONS

❶ Make for the gate near the entrance to the Seven Sisters Country Park and follow the grassy path towards the beach. The path gradually curves to the right, running alongside a concrete track. Continue between the track and the Cuckmere River and make for a South Downs Way sign.

### ② IN THE AREA

If you have the time, take a look at the Seaford Head Nature Reserve, which lies on the west side of Cuckmere Haven. This chalk headland, which rises 282ft (86m) above the sea, is a popular local attraction and from here the coastal views are magnificent.

### ❧ ON THE WALK

Shingle plants thrive on the sheltered parts of beaches and a stroll at Cuckmere Haven reveals the yellow horned-poppy and the fleshy leaved sea kale. Sea beet, curled dock and scentless chamomile can also be found here.

❷ Avoid the long distance trail as it runs in from the left, pass it and the Foxhole campsite and keep ahead, through the gate towards the beach. Veer left at the beach and South Downs Way sign. On reaching the next gate, don't go through it. Instead, keep right and follow the beach sign. Pass a couple of wartime pill boxes on the left and go through a gate. Join a stony path and walk ahead to the beach, with the white wall of the Seven Sisters rearing up beside you.

❸ Turn right and cross the shore, approaching a Cuckmere Haven Emergency Point sign. Branch off to the right to join another track here. Follow this for about 50yds (46m) until you come to a junction and keep left, following the Park Trail. Keep beside the Cuckmere; the landscape here is characterised by a network of meandering channels and waterways, all feeding into the river. Pass a turning for Foxhole campsite and follow the footpath as it veers left, in line with the Cuckmere. Make for a kissing gate and continue on the straight path by the side of the river.

❹ Keep ahead to the road at Exceat Bridge and on the left is the Golden Galleon pub. Turn right and follow the A259 to return to the car park at the country park.

### ⑪ EATING AND DRINKING

The Golden Galleon by Exceat Bridge is a very popular 18th-century inn thought to have inspired Rudyard Kipling's poem 'Song of the Smugglers'. The menu is traditional and very British, with various other dishes. The visitor centre at the Seven Sisters Country Park has a restaurant and tea rooms and in summer there is often an ice cream van in the car park.

The white cliffs of The Seven Sisters

# VIRGINIA WOOLF AND THE RIVER OUSE

Where the River Ouse cuts through the Downs, through two beautiful villages with important literary associations.

In 1919 the novelist Virginia Woolf and her husband, Leonard, leading lights in the Bloomsbury Group, bought Monk's House in Rodmell as a country retreat. Frequent visitors included T S Eliot and E M Forster. A modest weatherboarded cottage, the Woolfs extended Monk's House and Virginia used a timber lodge at the bottom of the garden for her writing.

The Woolfs may have followed Virginia's sister to Sussex, for in 1916 Vanessa Bell moved to Charleston Farmhouse, nearer Eastbourne, also now open to the public, but certainly Virginia worked on many of her best-known novels at Monk's Wood. Besides the creativity of her writing and her life here with Leonard, Monk's House is inevitably associated with Virginia's sad death in 1941. Subject to depression and melancholia all her life, she drowned herself in the River Ouse, having first filled her pockets with stones.

Leonard Woolf lived on here until his death in 1969 and Monk's House was given to the National Trust in 1980. Lived in full time by tenants the house is open to visitors on Wednesday and Saturday afternoons between April and October, the visit including Virginia Woolf's writing lodge.

### The Round Tower and the Ouse Valley

Southease's church has a round bell tower, one of three in Sussex. The other two are in Lewes (Walk 12) and Piddinghoe a mile and a half further south along the Ouse. These are a mere outcrop as most round towers are in East Anglia where there are about 170. Both areas are short of good building stone and round towers need no costly corners and edges in dressed stone and they mostly date from about 1000 to 1200.

These marshes with occasional islands such as Lower Rise in The Brooks nearer Lewes were taken in hand in the 1530s by the local gentry and the river channelled between dyke banks and drainage channels cut. The sea had invaded in the Great Storm of 1421 that caused enormous devastation and floods in Sussex and almost drowned Holland. Part of this work included cutting a new channel to the sea which emerged at a 'new haven' or harbour, now Newhaven and not so new.

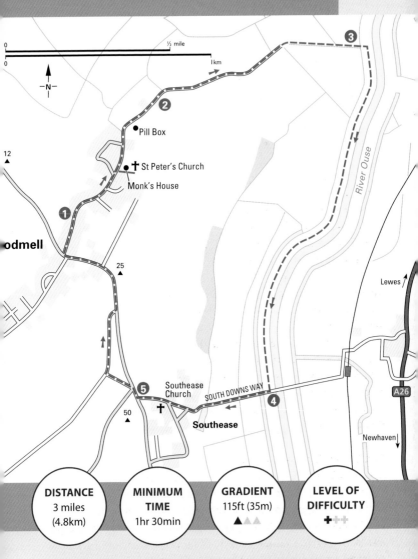

½ mile

1 km

—N—

Pill Box

† St Peter's Church

Monk's House

12 ▲

**odmell**

25 ▲

River Ouse

Lewes ↑

Southease Church

SOUTH DOWNS WAY

50 ▲

**Southease**

A26

Newhaven ↓

**DISTANCE**
3 miles
(4.8km)

**MINIMUM TIME**
1hr 30min

**GRADIENT**
115ft (35m)
▲▲▲

**LEVEL OF DIFFICULTY**
+++

**PATHS** Tracks and river bank path, village streets and some lanes, 1 stile
**LANDSCAPE** Water-meadows of the River Ouse and villages on the foothills
of the South Downs **SUGGESTED MAP** OS Explorer 122 Brighton & Hove
**START/FINISH** Grid reference: TQ 420062
**DOG FRIENDLINESS** On lead along road between Southease and Rodmell
and in Rodmell village **PARKING** In Rodmell's village street or at car park beyond
Monk's House when the house is not open **PUBLIC TOILETS** None on route

## WALK 11 DIRECTIONS

❶ Walk along Rodmell's village street, diverting to visit the church, and pass Monk's House where Virginia and Leonard Woolf lived. At the village/National Trust car park at the end of the village continue ahead at the bridleway sign onto a metalled track.

> 🍴 **EATING AND DRINKING**
>
> The Abergavenny Arms pub in Rodmell prides itself on home-cooked, locally produced food and does cream teas on Wednesday and Saturday afternoons in the season.

❷ Beyond a water treatment works you are in the flat water-meadows of the River Ouse where it cuts through the chalk of the South Downs, with long views to Lewes Castle (Walk 12) and cattle and horses grazing. Continue ahead and through a bridle gate, probably disturbing a heron or two, then pass through another bridle gate to reach the river bank.

❸ Ascend the river bank flood dyke and, through the kissing gate, go right to walk downstream, the tidal Ouse beside you. Continue alongside as it winds gently towards the sea and at Southease Bridge go through two bridle gates and turn right on to the South Downs Way National Trail. (At the time of writing, autumn 2010, the Trail crosses the river on a temporary footbridge while the main bridge is rebuilt).

❹ Follow the lane and beyond a line of willows leave the water-meadows to climb to Southease, a small and pretty village with a green and a church with a Norman round tower and nave and 13th-century wall paintings. Continue on the lane uphill to the junction with the main road.

❺ Bear right along the metalled pavement and shortly go left to follow the South Downs Way sign going right through a bridle gate. Follow the guideposts to descend into a valley and through a bridle gate. At the valley bottom leave the South Downs Way, which bears left, and continue ahead on a track running parallel to the road to Rodmell. At the main road, cross over to reach a metalled pavement and then follow the road into Rodmell and the end of the walk.

> 🔎 **IN THE AREA**
>
> Newhaven Fort, perched on the chalk bluffs above Newhaven is now open to the public every day between March and October. There is much to see and do, including a recreated Blitz bomb shelter, guns, tunnels and ramparts. The current fort, built in the 1860s during yet another French invasion scare, is the last in a line of forts stretching back to Roman times.

# LEWES AND DEMOCRACY

A walk through this fine county town on a slightly unusual route that gives a flavour of its long history.

Lewes is the county town of East Sussex and has the necessary accoutrements of a fine stone County Hall of 1808 and a gaol. Its ridge-top setting and architecture reflects a long history. Many of the buildings survive from the Middle Ages, including several parish churches, a great castle, which unusually had two mottes, an oddity shared with Lincoln, and 13th-century town walls in stone. There are many medieval and Tudor houses in the town, including Anne of Cleves House in Southover and stone mansions such as Southover Grange. Great wealth returned in the 18th century and many older houses were refronted in brick or mathematical tiles, a hanging tile that looks like brick. A good example is the pair of tiles near The Barbican.

### A Priory, a Castle and a Battle

In Southover are the remains of the great Cluniac Priory of St Pancras, which was ruthlessly cut through and partly destroyed by the railway. To the north of the priory are the remains of the gatehouse, while to the south are the monastic buildings and fragments of the abbey church. Founded by William de Warenne, Earl of Surrey, in 1077, after a visit to the great mother abbey of Cluny in Burgundy, the Priory was one of the wealthiest in England until destroyed in the Dissolution of the Monasteries in 1537.

The castle dominates views for miles around and was also founded by William de Warenne around 1100. Unusually, there are two mottes or mounds with a bailey linking them, part of which is the old tiltyard. The south west motte is crowned by the current Norman shell keep while the north east one is largely hidden by buildings.

In 1264 the royal army of King Henry III was defeated by rebels led by Simon de Montfort outside Lewes, the King watching from the castle. Defeated, Henry conceded and the English Parliament was born.

Simon was an unlikely champion of the forerunner of our democracy and a pretty unsavoury character. French born he was the son of the ruthless leader of the Albigensian Crusade and was eventually killed at the Battle of Evesham in August 1265, universally hated by his former allies.

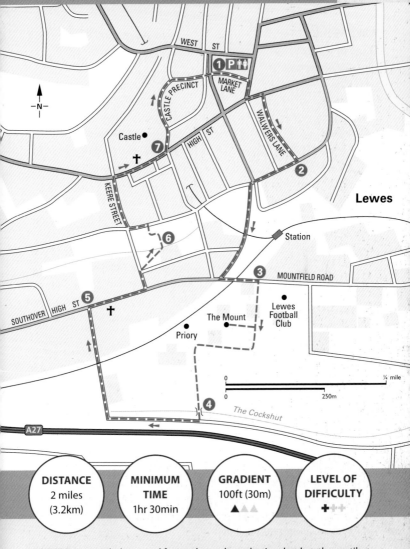

| DISTANCE | MINIMUM TIME | GRADIENT | LEVEL OF DIFFICULTY |
|---|---|---|---|
| 2 miles (3.2km) | 1hr 30min | 100ft (30m) ▲▲▲ | +++ |

**PATHS** Town roads, lanes and footpaths, parks and a river bank path, no stiles
**LANDSCAPE** Mostly townscape with a foray into the town's water-meadows
**SUGGESTED MAP** OS Explorer 122 Brighton & Hove
**START/FINISH** Grid reference: TQ 415101
**DOG FRIENDLINESS** On lead in town and in parks
**PARKING** West Street pay-and-display car park
**PUBLIC TOILETS** West Street Car Park

*Opposite: A cobbled street in the historic town of Lewes*

## WALK 12 DIRECTIONS

❶ Leave the West Street Car Park by The Crown Inn and bear left into Market Lane. Then go right towards the war memorial. Here go left downhill in High Street and shortly right into Walwers Lane and descend this narrow lane to its end.

❷ Turn right along a road, Lansdowne Place, and at the crossroads go left to pass the railway station and left into Mountfield Road.

---

### 🍴 EATING AND DRINKING

There are plenty of pubs and cafés in Lewes, including by the car park The Needlemakers, a former candle factory built in 1821. It was converted into a specialist shopping centre in 1984 and has a friendly café.

---

❸ Turn right just before Lewes Football Club and in the park walk up the spiral path onto the summit of The Mount. From the summit you can see the ruins of Lewes Priory (inaccessible and undergoing major restoration at time of writing). Return to the path and go right alongside a wall, then left along football pitches to a footbridge.

❹ Cross the footbridge to bear right alongside The Cockshut stream. At the end of the river go right onto a lane and then immediately right to pass under a railway bridge. Just before this there is a now closed access to the Priory for a view of the ruins. Continue to the main road, Southover High Street.

❺ Turn right and pass by St John the Baptist Church, which is the remains of Lewes Priory's 13th-century north gate. Go left at The King's Head and shortly half right into the grounds of a mansion, Southover Grange.

❻ Cross a footbridge and leave the park to the right of the house and go left along the road, then right up a very steep cobbled lane, Keere Street. Emerge by The Fifteenth Century Bookshop and turn right into High Street, passing St Michael's Church with its rare round tower (see Walk 11).

❼ Go left into Castle Gate, actually a lane, and having visited the castle pass through the 14th-century Barbican tower and then the Norman gateway. Pause at the information board relating to the Battle of Lewes. Ignore Castle Banks and continue downhill along Castle Precinct towards Castle Ditch Lane and into an alley that emerges by The Lamb of Lewes pub. Continue ahead into Market Lane.

---

### 🔍 IN THE AREA

If you feel like a stiff climb rewarded by wonderful views ascend Mount Caburn on the Lewes Downs east of the Ouse. At the summit are the earthworks of an Iron Age hill-fort, paragliders leaping off to soar and the Ouse Brooks spread far below.

---

# A MILLER'S TALE

Walk amid echoes of long gone watermills
and along the banks of the winding River Ouse.

Apart from the hamlet's name, the bridges, fast flowing weirs and sluices
are the only real clues that there were once large watermills here. Some are
millstreams and some are mill-races. Burned down in 1939, the oil mills and
button factory buildings have long gone, leaving only their diverted and
controlled watercourses, in fact the much divided River Ouse. This was also
where the Ouse ceases to be a tidal river but the area is still prone to flooding.

## The Millers of Barcombe

It is thought there were watermills here as early as Roman times but they
were first recorded in the *Domesday Book*. During the 19th century, the mills
produced flour and vegetable oil from locally grown crops and another was a
button mill. These buttons were produced from what is known as vegetable
ivory (no elephants or walruses involved). They utilised the nuts from the
ivory-nut palm and similar species of palm imported from South America, in
particular the Amazon basin, but also from trees growing along the banks
of tropical rivers from Panama to Peru. The water-powered machinery was
used to cut and shape and decorate this ivory-like nut. What many people
think are old ivory buttons are not. The last mill was reconstructed in 1870
and some were converted to be turbine driven mills, but a disastrous fire in
1939 brought many centuries of milling history to an abrupt end, as they were
never rebuilt.

## Barcombe Mills station

At Point ❸ are the surviving buildings of the station, mainly built to serve
the watermills and also anglers fishing for trout in the River Ouse. This
was one of four stations on the Lewes and Uckfield Railway that opened
to traffic in 1858. Isfield is the next station north (see Walk 14). The line
closed in 1969 but little happened to the station buildings until the 1980s.
Briefly a restaurant, the buildings are now homes but their former use is still
recognisable. On the north side of the road a British Railways notice board
survives in Southern Region green.

# Walk 13

# Barcombe Mills

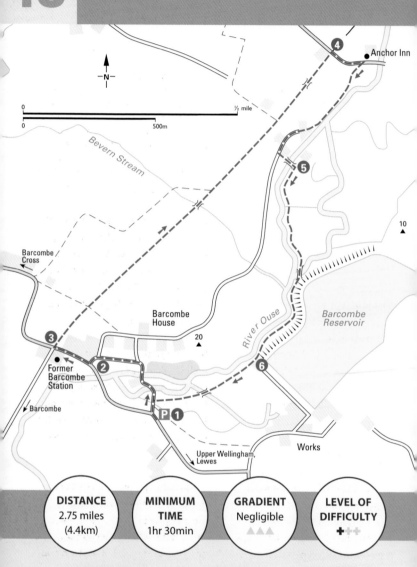

**DISTANCE**
2.75 miles
(4.4km)

**MINIMUM TIME**
1hr 30min

**GRADIENT**
Negligible

**LEVEL OF DIFFICULTY**

**PATHS** Riverside paths, a former railway line track bed, 1 stile
**LANDSCAPE** River banks and the course of a dismantled railway
**SUGGESTED MAPS** OS Explorer 122 Brighton & Hove or 123 Eastbourne
& Beachy Head **START/FINISH** Grid reference: TQ 434146
**DOG FRIENDLINESS** On lead in livestock fields
**PARKING** Public car park on Barcombe Mills Road, off the A26
**PUBLIC TOILETS** None on route

## WALK 13 DIRECTIONS

**1** From the car park the path passes an ancient oak to bear right onto a lane. Cross three bridges, the third across two sluices. The lane winds right across what is reputed to be Sussex's first toll bridge and, over a last bridge, goes left onto a metalled lane past houses. This becomes a path to join a through road.

**2** Continue along the road to reach the former buildings of Barcombe railway station.

**3** Here turn right onto a licenced bridleway, signed 'Anchor Lane', which heads towards the next station at Isfield (Walk 14). Follow the trackbed, cross a stream on a railway bridge and where the track bears left towards some cottages keep ahead on a path through trees, still on the trackbed and cross another old railway bridge.

**4** Emerging at a lane bear right. At the Anchor Inn, go right onto a footpath at the footpath sign just before the bridge over the River Ouse. Go through a kissing gate beside sluices and continue ahead along the river bank, the gate with a reminder about dogs being kept on leads. Through a gate

> **EATING AND DRINKING**
> The Anchor Inn is at the half-way point by the River Ouse. It does food and you can also hire rowing boats and canoes here. There is also the Royal Oak at Barcombe Cross that does lunch and evening meals, has a skittle alley and serves Harveys ales.

continue alongside a lesser branch of the river and pass a pill box. Through another gate the path bears left across a drive and through a small gate into a field of cattle. Follow a lane and beyond a farm building go left across the river on a bridge.

**5** Bearing right to walk along the opposite river bank, the main river merges from the left at a kissing gate. Cross a footbridge, the path now along the opposite bank of the main river, the embankment of Barcombe Reservoir to your left.

**6** Through a kissing gate continue along the river bank and cross a footbridge with a gate at each end. Over it bear right past another pill box. At a step through stile go left and along the lane back to the car park.

> **IN THE AREA**
> A stone's throw south of Barcombe is Wellingham Herb Garden. Here an 18th-century walled kitchen garden has been turned into a delightful and fragrant herb garden, its main section set out as a parterre with a lion statue in the centre. Open at weekends between April and September, it grows more than 150 varieties of herbs and has a herb nursery and a shop.

# A MEDIEVAL CHURCH AND A VICTORIAN RAILWAY

See a heritage steam railway in action, walk in delightful Sussex countryside and alongside the winding River Uck.

### Lavender and Locomotives

Walk 13 followed part of the course of the former Lewes to Uckfield Railway line, which opened in 1858 and by 1860 had been absorbed into the London, Brighton and South Coast Railway. Ending its days as part of British Railways, supporters successfully fought off Dr Beeching's closure proposals. However, it was a short lived victory because it was finally closed in 1969.

Thus matters stood until 1983 when the station was bought and restoration of the station buildings and the signal box was undertaken, and new railway track was laid. There are 1.75 miles (1.2km) of track running north from the station and the walk route passes over it, giving a good view of the station. Now owned by the Lavender Line Preservation Society, the name is nothing to do with the scented plant but was the name of local coal merchants, A E Lavender & Sons, who operated from the station goods yard. Possibly the choice of name was influenced by the nearby Bluebell Line.

Besides visiting and being hauled by steam or diesel you could even enrol for driver training courses. The Cinders Buffet at the station is popular and the railway runs Wine and Dine Trains where you eat on the move. There is also a model railway in Lavender & Sons old coal office and a coach with displays and old photographs of the line in its heyday. Always fascinating, this is a well run heritage railway. For timetables and other details visit their website (but it is generally open at weekends).

### A Remote Church

St Margaret of Antioch parish church is out in the fields near Isfield Place while the village centre has migrated to the railway line. The church has a Norman tower and in the chapel are a collection of superb monuments to the Shurley Family of Isfield Place; one Sir John who died in 1527 is described as 'chef clerke of the kechen to our souayn kyng henry ye viii', that is Cofferer or keeper of the kitchen budget to King Henry VIII. To the west of the church, amid trees, are the earthworks of a Norman motte-and-bailey castle overlooking the River Ouse.

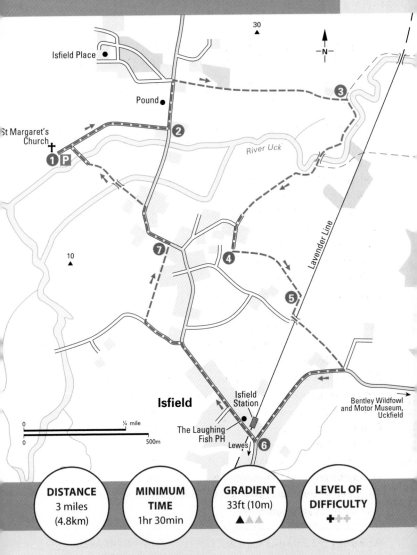

Isfield Place
Pound
St Margaret's Church
❶ P
River Uck
30 ▲
—N—
❸
❷
❼
10 ▲
❹
❺
Lavender Line
Isfield
Isfield Station
The Laughing Fish PH
Lewes
❻
Bentley Wildfowl and Motor Museum, Uckfield

0        ¼ mile
0        500m

**DISTANCE**
3 miles
(4.8km)

**MINIMUM TIME**
1hr 30min

**GRADIENT**
33ft (10m)
▲ ▲ ▲

**LEVEL OF DIFFICULTY**
✚ ✚ ✚

**PATHS** Field paths, tracks and lanes, 10 stiles
**LANDSCAPE** Gently rolling countryside and the banks of the River Uck
**SUGGESTED MAPS** OS Explorer 122 Brighton & Hove or 123 Eastbourne & Beachy Head **START/FINISH** Grid reference: TQ 444180
**DOG FRIENDLINESS** On lead in livestock fields and through village
**PARKING** Car park at Isfield church, but not on Sunday mornings when always full for church services **PUBLIC TOILETS** None on route

**WALK 14 DIRECTIONS**

❶ From the church car park walk back along the access lane to pass a Sussex pill box.

---

### 🍴 EATING AND DRINKING

The Cinders Buffet at Isfield Station is noted for its breakfasts and also does hot and cold meals and refreshments. Next to the station is The Laughing Fish pub which has cask ales and home-made food.

---

❷ At the road junction bear left and pass the walled pound. Opposite the gates to Isfield Place, go right over a footbridge and stile and keep ahead. Bear left to a stile and continue within a copse to a stile. Over this head half right across pasture to climb a stile in the far corner. Bear right along a grassy track and, over a stile, keep ahead towards white field gates.

❸ Go right and through a gate to follow the river bank to a bridge with gates each side. Across this go right along the river bank and through a gate. Through a hedge gap go left alongside a hedge, away from the river. Keep ahead through a gate and over a footbridge to cross a paddock to a stile. Keep ahead to pass between the buildings of Rowebuck Stud.

❹ Go left at a footpath post beyond and over a stile to continue ahead past a garden, then quarter right across a field to the railway.

❺ Bear right alongside the railway, then through a kissing gate, cross the railway bridge with views to Isfield Station. Over a stile continue ahead and onto the lane via a stile. Turn right and follow the road to the level crossing in Isfield.

❻ Turn right to visit the Lavender Line based in Isfield Station and then continue ahead along the village street as far as a bend to go left at the footpath sign. Follow a lane as it curves right. Where it bears left cross a stile and continue ahead to a kissing gate. At the village hall field bear quarter left to the road.

❼ Bear left along the road and then left onto a footpath opposite Hope Cottage. Through a gate continue ahead across sheep pasture, Isfield church ahead. Through a hand gate cross the River Uck on a footbridge, then go through a bridle gate. Cross another footbridge into a cattle pasture and go half left to a kissing gate by the church.

---

### ⌖ IN THE AREA

If you haven't had enough of steam railways visit Bentley Wildfowl and Motor Museum a couple of miles south-east of Isfield where, among many other attractions, there is a miniature steam railway. There is also a wildfowl reserve, a fine motor museum, an ancient buildings trail, formal gardens and refreshments.

---

# THE FIRST HERITAGE STEAM RAILWAY

From a heathland common pass the Bluebell Railway's southern terminus and walk alongside the River Ouse.

The walk passes the entrance to the southern terminus of the Bluebell Railway that runs for 9.5 miles (15km) through the prettiest Sussex countryside towards East Grinstead. This pioneer of preserved steam locomotion and heritage railways celebrated its golden jubilee in 2010. It still has ambitions and will soon reach East Grinstead to link up with the national network.

Originally opened in 1882 as the Lewes and East Grinstead Railway, it carried passengers as well as agricultural produce, milk, coal and timber. Its last years under British Railways in the 1950s were bitter with locals vigorously fighting closure, eventually in vain as the line was finally closed in 1958. The Lewes and East Grinstead Railway Preservation Society was set up, soon renamed the Bluebell Railway, and after much hard work the first train arrived at Sheffield Park Station in May 1960. It was the first preserved standard gauge passenger railway not just in England but also in the whole world, indeed the doyen of the heritage railway movement.

Since then it has expanded its steam locomotive stock from two small tank engines to over 20, including top link express locomotives. Being situated in the old Southern Railway area it focuses on locomotives, carriages and wagons from that region, as you would expect, but it is a wonderful day out and runs services almost all the year round.

### Wowo and Wapsbourne

You pass Wapsbourne farmhouse whose farm buildings and southern fields are used by the camping organisation Wowo. Their shelters range from tepees and Mongolian yurts to more conventional tents.

Wapsbourne farmhouse itself is one of those tall picturesque Sussex farmhouses with square panel timber framing, timber mullioned windows with old leaded lights and a roof clad in Horsham stone slabs. These are a tremendous weight when compared with roof tiles and require a robust roof and frame to support them. The whole ensemble of this 16th-century farmhouse with its massive 17th-century brick chimneystacks is highly evocative of the superb yeoman houses that dot the Weald.

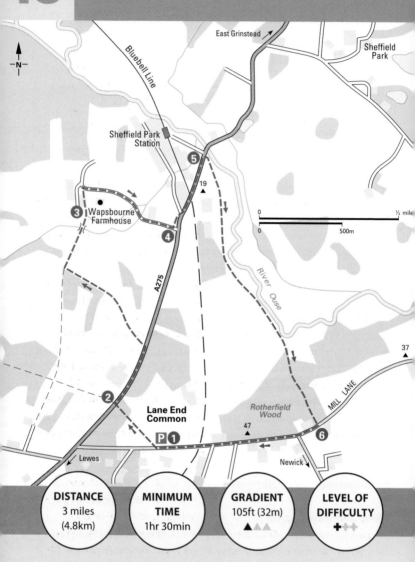

East Grinstead

Sheffield Park

Bluebell Line

Sheffield Park Station

**5**

**3** Wapsbourne Farmhouse

**4**

▲ 19

A275

River Ouse

▲ 37

MILL LANE

**2**

**Lane End Common**

P **1**

Rotherfield Wood

▲ 47

**6**

Lewes

Newick

—N—

0 ........ ½ mile
0 ........ 500m

| DISTANCE | MINIMUM TIME | GRADIENT | LEVEL OF DIFFICULTY |
|---|---|---|---|
| 3 miles (4.8km) | 1hr 30min | 105ft (32m) ▲▲▲ | +++ |

**PATHS** Paths through fields and commons, short stretches of road and lane, 2 stiles **LANDSCAPE** Heathland, rolling countryside and the valley of the River Ouse **SUGGESTED MAP** OS Explorer 135 Ashdown Forest **START/FINISH** Grid reference: TQ 403221 **DOG FRIENDLINESS** On lead in livestock fields and along roads and lanes, particularly the A275 **PARKING** Lane End Common car park **PUBLIC TOILETS** None on route

## WALK 15 DIRECTIONS

❶ From the car park on Lane End Common cross the footbridge in its north west corner and continue on the path to the left of a sign. Cross grass and bear quarter left alongside woodland, entering the woods a little way along to continue. Emerging from this, cross another grassy area and re-enter bracken and scrub woodland. Follow this path to emerge at the A275.

❷ Turn right along the road, ignoring the footpath opposite, and passing Lane End Farm continue to a stile on the left. Over this into pasture, cross to a gate then head for the right-hand corner of woods across the field. Go through a hand gate and down steps, the path then continuing along the woodland edge. Reaching a footpath sign at a track go right amid lines of trees, lime, hornbeam and beech, continuing ahead to cross a bridge.

❸ This is the Wowo Campsite. Keep ahead and go to the right of a barn and weave through the farmyard, noting the timber-framed Wapsbourne farmhouse on your right. Past this go right and along a metalled track.

> ### 🍴 EATING AND DRINKING
> On the route, the only refreshment available is the Bluebell Railway at Sheffield Park Station. Here there is a restaurant and The Bessemer Arms with lunches and snacks.

❹ Just before the road, the A275, bear left to walk inside the field and parallel to the road. At the end go down steps and continue along the road as far as the entrance to the Bluebell Railway.

❺ Opposite this go right to descend steps and over a stile, signposted 'Sussex Ouse Valley Way'. The path roughly follows the banks of the River Ouse but cuts out many of its meanders. Through a gate and over a footbridge the path veers right and into Rotherfield Wood. Continue ahead on a clear track through a wood. Ascend to the crest and pass between gates to a road, via a hand gate.

❻ Turn right to follow Mill Lane and at a junction continue ahead, signposted 'Sheffield Park', Rotherfield Wood on your right. Cross the overgrown trackbed and continue to the car park.

> ### 🌳 IN THE AREA
> Just past the Bluebell Railway is Sheffield Park Garden, historic parkland originally landscaped by 'Capability Brown' and then by Humphrey Repton in the 18th century and further developed in the 20th century. It has four lakes, an arboretum and rhododendrons. Now National Trust, the parkland and gardens are open all the year, the gardens only at weekends in January and February.

# AT THE GATES OF ASHDOWN FOREST

Explore the village of Forest Row, walk an old railway line and see a splendid 17th-century ruined mansion.

Most small settlements, which grew up on the edge of the Ashdown Forest, were clumps of sporadic cottages straggling into hamlets. Forest Row, unusually, was developed as a single street of houses or 'row'.

By the mid-19th century, Forest Row was a hamlet with a few houses, around a green, and a parish church dating from 1836. Built as a chapel of ease within the then parish of East Grinstead, Forest Row did not become a full independent parish until 1894. This was probably in recognition of the village's expansion after the East Grinstead and Tunbridge Wells Railway station opened in 1866.

## Freshfield Hall

Perhaps the most flamboyant building in the village is Freshfield Hall, which faces south behind a small triangular green with a good war memorial. Built for the village in 1892, for Henry Freshfield of nearby Kidbrooke Park, it is in local Sussex style with ornate plasterwork in the gable and around the memorial tablet to his son who died in 1891. The architect was a Scotsman, John M Brydon, who pulled out all the stops for his patron.

## Old Brambletye House

After leaving the railway trackbed you pass the ruins of Brambletye House. Here there are three surviving three storey towers and bits of the linking walls, the central entrance tower with the date '1631' in a lozenge above and the southern tower retaining its leaded ogee roof. This is the front elevation of the house, the sides and rear having long been demolished. It was evidently built in the local sandstone and had large mullioned windows. The ruins are set back from the lane and fronted by the remains of the gatehouse.

It was built for Sir Henry Compton who died about 1649, a lawyer who through his connections with the powerful Sackvilles of East Grinstead, was appointed a ranger of Ashdown Forest, a Justice of the Peace and Member of Parliament for East Grinstead. However, it seems that Brambletye was abandoned by the end of the 17th century.

**DISTANCE**
2.5 miles
(4km)

**MINIMUM TIME**
1hr 15min

**GRADIENT**
50ft (15m)
▲▲▲

**LEVEL OF DIFFICULTY**
✚✚✚

**PATHS** Pavements in Forest Row, a former railway trackbed, lanes and field paths, 6 stiles **LANDSCAPE** Rolling countryside and the headwaters of the River Medway **SUGGESTED MAP** OS Explorer 135 Ashdown Forest
**START/FINISH** Grid reference: TQ 426349
**DOG FRIENDLINESS** On lead in Forest Row and in livestock fields around Burnthouse Farm
**PARKING** Car park on Hartfield Road **PUBLIC TOILETS** None on route

# Walk
## 16
# Forest Row

## WALK 16 DIRECTIONS

❶ From the car park cross Hartfield Road via the pedestrian crossing. Continue to the left of the shops onto a path, Forester's Link. Follow this round to the right and go left at the sculptured tree stump. The path skirts a timber yard and crosses a stream, the upper reaches of the River Medway, on a footbridge. Continue to a signboard for the Forest Way Country Park.

❷ At the signboard go left and follow the footpath, signed 'National Cycle Network 21'. Ascend, then bear left onto a lane which runs alongside an old tree covered railway embankment and follow it to the main road, the A22.

❸ Cross the road via pedestrian crossing lights and go up a tarmac path to join the railway trackbed, now a cycle and foot path and part of the Forest Way waymarked route.

❹ At Brambletye Crossing leave the trackbed path and go left onto a lane. The lane bears right and passes the fascinating ruins of Old Brambletye House. Continue past the gatehouse remains and the 17th-century stone boundary wall. Pass the gates to Brambletye Manor Farmhouse and go left onto a track. To your right is the site of Brambletye House's predecessor. Cross a stone bridge over the Medway whose upper reaches were dammed in the 1950s to form Weir Wood Reservoir 0.5 miles (800m) to your right.

❺ At the footpath crossroads go left over a stile. Continue with a young oak wood on your right, cross a stile into a field and bear half right, leaving the river bank, towards a timber-framed farmhouse, Burnthouse Farm. Over a stile ascend towards the house and barn. At the barn, go left and over a stile and bear right to another two stiles. Over a stile, bear left to continue alongside the left-hand hedge in pasture. Cross a stile and continue within scrub, the path meandering through to a footbridge. Cross this, winding along a shingle path beside the stream to emerge in the car park of a block of flats. Pass beneath the flats and shops, up two flights of steps to Lewes Road, back in Forest Row.

> ### 🍽 EATING AND DRINKING
> There are several pubs and restaurants in Forest Row, including the Chequers Inn Hotel, which does good bar snack meals. The Swan opposite the Village Hall has a varied menu but is pricier.

❻ Bear right towards the spiky spire of the parish church of Holy Trinity, a modest stone building of 1836. Beyond the tile-hung and timber-framed Chequers Inn Hotel cross the road at the pedestrian lights and continue ahead behind the village hall to bear right along the quieter lane, Hillside, and then turn left down Hartfield Road to return to the car park.

# A GREEN LUNG FOR CRAWLEY

This fine park has many good paths, lakes and varied landscapes as well as attractions such as the Nature Centre.

Originally within the Worth Forest held by William de Warenne, Earl of Surrey, whose name keeps cropping up in any history of Sussex (see Walk 12), Tilgate was separated out from the forest and by the 16th century a mansion apparently existed, but nearer the main lake.

In the 1860s, John Nix bought the estate and set about reconstructing it. On the site now occupied by the empty pub, he built a large Tudor-style stone mansion with many gables and chimneystacks. He and his successors planted the pinetum and kitchen garden, which is now the walled garden. The estate was broken up in the 1930s and the lakes were bought by Sir Malcolm Campbell to develop Bluebird for the world-speed record attempt. There is a blue commemorative plaque by the lake.

## Public Space

In 1964, Crawley Urban District Council bought the estate and turned it into today's park, a much used and much loved 'green lung' for Crawley. In the designation of Crawley as a new town under the 1949 New Town Act, 200 acres (81ha) of the Tilgate Estate was zoned as public open space but not purchased until 15 years later.

Unfortunately Nix's mansion was in too poor a state to retain and was demolished, but the stable block survives and has since been converted to flats. The modern pub is currently un-let at the time of writing, but the rest is thriving with a very popular Walled Garden and Nature Centre. The great gales of 1987 severely damaged the Victorian pinetum (collection of specimen conifer trees that you pass through) but this is being restored.

## A Dam Diversion

The route between Points ❶ and ❷ is in effect a diversion due to the works currently under way to raise Tilgate Lake's dam by 8ft (2.5m) as part of wider flood defences for Crawley. This work should be completed by summer 2011 when presumably you will be able to walk along the dam and fishermen and boats will return to the lake.

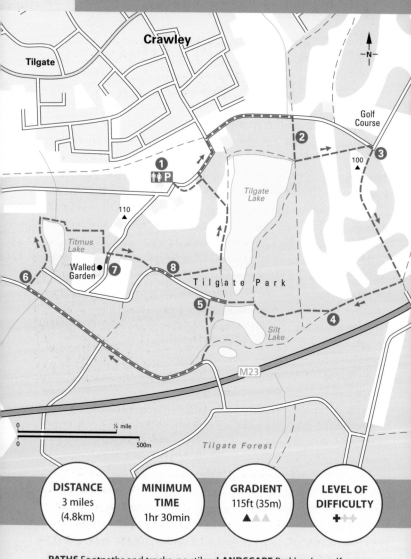

|  | DISTANCE | MINIMUM TIME | GRADIENT | LEVEL OF DIFFICULTY |
|---|---|---|---|---|
|  | 3 miles (4.8km) | 1hr 30min | 115ft (35m) ▲▲▲ | +++ |

**PATHS** Footpaths and tracks, no stiles **LANDSCAPE** Parkland, a golf course, woods including a Victorian pinetum and lakes

**SUGGESTED MAP** OS Explorer 134 Crawley & Horsham

**START/FINISH** Grid reference: TQ 275345

**DOG FRIENDLINESS** Dog friendly

**PARKING** Tilgate Park Car Park, pay at entry barrier

**PUBLIC TOILETS** At the car park and in the Walled Garden

## WALK 17 DIRECTIONS

**1** From the car park cross the road towards the children's play area. Pass to its left and at cross paths bear left, then right just before an emergency car parking area to descend parallel to the road. Skirt the chain link fence, then go right onto the road. Follow this road and cross a bridge over a stream, then go right alongside the stream.

**2** Nearing the dam bear left onto a gravelly track and where it bears right at the corner of the lake continue ahead on a path through trees. Emerge from the trees onto a golf course and cross three fairways to a footpath sign.

**3** Go right at the footpath sign and follow a track across two fairways and woodland strips. The path curves left into woods, crosses a third fairway and almost immediately bears right onto a path within a tree belt. Cross three fairways and continue into woods.

**4** At a path crossroads keep ahead on either path to descend to the main track where you bear right to descend. At the valley floor bear left over a footbridge and along the dam of the Silt Lake. At the end continue on the second path from the left amid pines. The path winds within the Pinetum as far as a timber footbridge.

**5** Don't cross but continue ahead on a grassy path amid more open specimen conifer trees. Ahead is the roar of the M23. Reaching the track near the motorway fence bear right and follow the track amid woods. Descend to the valley bottom, cross the stream and bear right to leave the track.

**6** The track winds along in woods beside Titmus Lake. At the end, go right along the dam path, then go right and left to continue ahead uphill with glimpses of alpacas and other animals through the hedge on your right.

> **ⓘ EATING AND DRINKING**
> Within Tilgate Park, the main refreshment area is the café in the Walled Garden. It serves snacks, sandwiches, baguettes, drinks and of course ice cream. Ice cream vans also visit the park: there is usually one at the main car park at weekends.

**7** At the crest go right towards the Nature Centre and left at a metal lion sculpture to a hand gate. Cross a lane and follow the tarmac path signed 'Footpath to Nature Centre, Craft Units, Walled Garden'. Visit the Walled Garden and then continue alongside its north wall. Go to the right of a bench across a grassy path and continue ahead on the path, curving right then left to a main wide path.

**8** Cross this, signed 'Peace Garden Path', Pinetum' but go half left down a greensward path amid trees heading to the lake edge. Go left alongside Tilgate Lake, then back uphill to the car park.

# HORSHAM'S COUNTRYSIDE AND DENNE PARK

Thanks to Denne Park you can soon be walking in the lush countryside south of Horsham.

Until Horsham was bypassed by the A24 it was a pretty unpleasant experience for motorists. The town has spread in all directions except mercifully south where fields are close by and Denne Park safeguards them for the future. In fact it was the creation of Denne Park in the 17th century that closed off the southern road into town. This means you can walk from the bustling town centre into The Causeway, a peaceful ancient street and mostly still lived in, to the church and then into the countryside.

This walk focuses on this southern end but the rest of the historic core has some excellent historic areas, particularly around The Carfax and the streets leading off it. Horsham was an important town and was first referred to as a borough in 1235. Until the 18th century the market was renowned for its poultry that were in great demand in London, particularly the four clawed Dorking breed; the town had an MP from 1295 onwards.

The town grew greatly after the railway arrived in 1848 spreading north across the former commons that had been enclosed in 1813, and flowing past Horsham Park with its mansion dating from the 1720s. Horsham Council bought the park and the mansion, which now houses the offices for the District Council while its grounds are a public park.

**Denne Park**

In about 1605, Sir Thomas Eversfields bought the Denne Park Estate and his family owned it until the 1940s. Judging by a date stone on the tower, Sir Thomas immediately built a new sandstone mansion to replace a medieval one that has vanished without trace. Much changed over the years and partly Georgianised it was restored closer to its 17th-century appearance in the 1870s. Now it has been converted to apartments but retains its long, grand entrance drive flanked by a double avenue of lime trees running some 650yds (594m) from the house to the road into Horsham. During the course of the 17th century the Eversfields converted much of their land to a deer park with a herd of fallow deer first mentioned in 1720. Indeed, there were still deer grazing the parkland into the 1930s.

*Opposite: St Mary's Church, The Causeway*

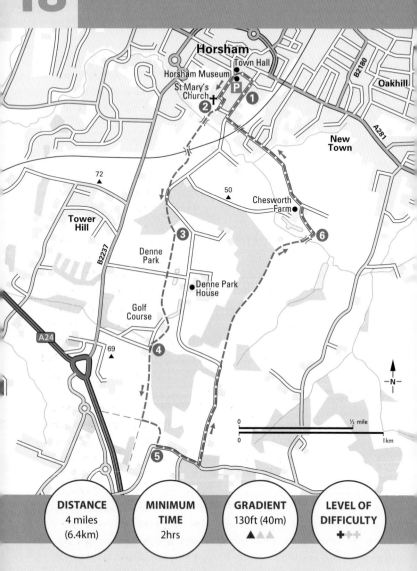

Horsham

Town Hall

Horsham Museum

St Mary's Church

**P**

**1**

**2** +

Oakhill

New Town

72 ▲

Chesworth Farm

50 ▲

Tower Hill

B2237

**3**

Denne Park

Denne Park House

**6**

A24

Golf Course

69 ▲

**4**

**5**

N

0          ½ mile
0                    1km

**DISTANCE**
4 miles
(6.4km)

**MINIMUM TIME**
2hrs

**GRADIENT**
130ft (40m)
▲ ▲▲

**LEVEL OF DIFFICULTY**
+ ++

**PATHS** Field paths, tracks and roads in Horsham, 4 stiles
**LANDSCAPE** Rolling countryside, former parkland, woods and some town lanes
**SUGGESTED MAP** OS Explorer 134 Crawley & Horsham
**START/FINISH** Grid reference: TQ 172303
**DOG FRIENDLINESS** Livestock only in the fields east of Hop Oast Farm
**PARKING** Denne Road pay-and-display car park
**PUBLIC TOILETS** Horsham Bus Station at the end of Black Horse Way

## WALK 18 DIRECTIONS

**1** From the car park turn left to the roundabout, bear left into East Street. At the crossroads go left and pass to the left of the battlemented and turreted Town Hall. Beyond you pass into The Causeway. It leads to the parish church, first passing Horsham Museum, a pale green rendered and gabled Tudor house.

**2** Skirt left of the parish church of St Mary and leave the churchyard on a path to the right of The Lodge to keep ahead across a footbridge, then alongside a cricket field to cross the railway line on a footbridge. Continue ahead past a footpath post, bearing half right to ascend to the corner of the field. Through the hedge gap continue ahead alongside a deep sunken way with the woods on your left. The path passes through the edge of the woods and through a ramshackle kissing gate emerging at crest level. Head for a footpath post ahead.

**3** Now in Denne Park bear quarter right from the footpath post to a kissing gate. Through this, cross the drive to Denne Park House enjoying the view of its façade, to a footpath post. Continue ahead across a golf course and at a footpath post bear half left to skirt the golf club buildings. Join the access drive beyond briefly before continuing ahead at a footpath post alongside a laurel hedge to a gravel parking area by a barn-like house.

**4** Continue ahead in a paddock and over a footbridge. Over a stile, cross to another by a gate. Over this cross the field to another stile, then another where you turn left into a hedged green lane, a public byway. Follow this as it bears right to a road.

**5** Bear left along the road past King's Farm and where the road bears right go left onto the public bridleway. Past a gate the lane becomes a footpath and crosses a field. Continue, now within the edge of Denne Park's woods. Continue ahead at a footpath junction to descend, just within the wood, continuing past two gates. At the next footpath post keep ahead, the path bearing right. Now between fields descend past lakes and cross a bridge.

**6** At the track junction go left signed 'public bridleway' and follow the track past Chesworth Farm. At a footpath sign bear left to continue along the lane, the church spire ahead. Continue ahead, cross a bridge over a stream, pass under a railway bridge, now in Chesworth Lane in the outskirts of Horsham. At Denne Road bear right and back to the car park.

---

**⑪ EATING AND DRINKING**

There is plenty of choice in Horsham. On the route in East Street there are numerous cafés and restaurants while round the Town Hall are several pubs, including The Bear Inn and the imposing Bar Vin, built in 1899.

# DEEP PASTURES OF THE SUSSEX WEALD

Enjoy a walk in pastoral Sussex with cattle grazing and oak trees in the hedges

Cowfold's name is fairly self-explanatory: there was a fold or enclosure for cattle, probably west of the church and it is known that the village was on one of Sussex's many drove roads along which cattle and sheep were herded towards mainly London but also other towns on the route. The fold was of course used for the manor's cattle as well. The earliest record of the village name is 'Cufaude' in 1255, becoming Cowfolde by 1589. Most of the inhabitants earned their living from farming the heavy Wealden clays until relatively recently, producing wheat and cattle, both dairy and beef. The parish is well wooded and in earlier times much was sold to the local iron masters for charcoal making or even to produce planking for ships.

The village is small with relatively little modern expansion and the best part is around the church with a row of houses on the north side turning their backs on the busy A281 and A272 and facing into the churchyard. This gives almost a cathedral close feel, albeit on a miniature scale of course. Some houses are timber-framed and 16th and 17th century in date, while there are also 18th- and 19th-century ones in brick or colour washed render. Several have the characteristic Horsham stone slab roofs and in the centre of the churchyard is the parish church of St Peter. Built in mellow golden sandstone with Horsham stone roof slabs, it sits very comfortably and is mostly Early English and Perpendicular Gothic. It has no spire, only a solid and battlemented west tower with a stair turret rising higher.

### St Hugh's Monastery

South of Cowfold is a very large monastery with a huge cloister court and a 203ft spire (62m) to its chapel, which you see at various points on the walk. This is a Carthusian monastery and the only one in England but because it is a reclusive monastic order you cannot visit. The first monastery built here since the 16th-century Reformation, the monks originally came from France and their architect was a Monsieur Norman from Calais. A robust example of French Victorian Gothic Revival, it was built between 1875 and 1883 and is something of a surprise to find it deep in the Sussex Weald.

30 ▲

**⑤**

**⑥**

↑ Crawley

A281

39 ▲

Browning's Farm

A272

West Grinstead, Billingshurst

**④**

Capon's Farm

St Peter's Church ✝

**Cowfold**

↑P① 

Haywards Heath

**②**

20 ▲

**③**

| 0 | | ½ mile |
| 0 | | 500m |

A281

↓ Henfield

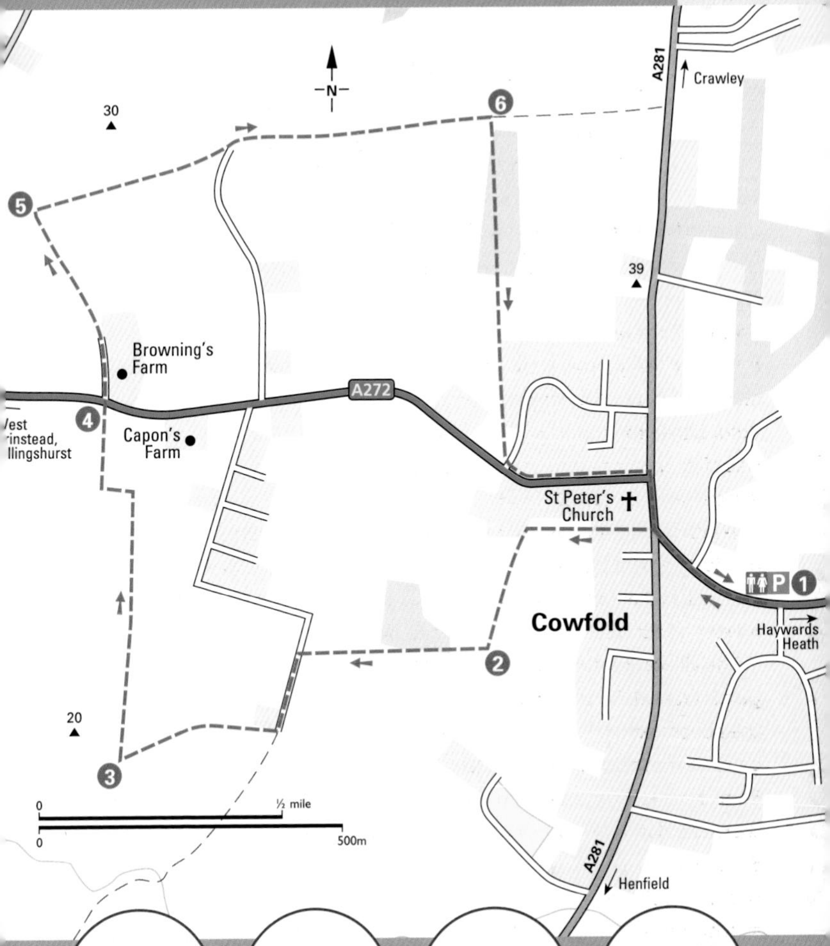

| DISTANCE | MINIMUM TIME | GRADIENT | LEVEL OF DIFFICULTY |
|----------|--------------|----------|---------------------|
| 2.5 miles (4km) | 1hr 15min | 50ft (15m) ▲▲▲ | ✚✚✚ |

**PATHS** Field paths and pavements in Cowfold village, 10 stiles
**LANDSCAPE** Gently rolling countryside, many oaks in hedges
**SUGGESTED MAP** OS Explorer 134 Crawley & Horsham
**START/FINISH** Grid reference: TQ 214225 **DOG FRIENDLINESS** On lead
in the village and in many of the fields where there are cattle
**PARKING** Cowfold Playing Fields car park, on A272 east of crossroads
**PUBLIC TOILETS** In the car park

## WALK 19 DIRECTIONS

❶ From the car park cross to the A272 and head right, passing the Village Hall of 1896. At the roundabout cross to the footpath into the churchyard passing between the Co-op and Cowfold Cottages. The path skirts to the left of the church and at the end bears right onto a footpath, soon crossing a stile. The path bears left by a school and runs between a post and wire fence and a thick hedge.

❷ At the end bear right through a gate, over a footbridge, then through another gate. Continue ahead along the field-edge, crossing a stile. At the corner of the field bear left to a stile near a tile-hung cottage. Over this stile pass the cottage and bear right over another stile into cattle pasture and continue ahead along the left-hand side of the hedge. Cross a footbridge and go half left across the next pasture.

❸ Reaching a stile do not cross but bear right alongside the hedge. Through a field gate continue ahead to the field corner. Here cross a plank footbridge, then go through a hand gate and turn right alongside the hedge. Cross a stile and continue ahead through a field gate, the chimneys of Capon's Farm to your right.

❹ Over a stile cross the A272 and keep ahead on the access lane to Browning's Farm and through a field gate. A gravel track skirts left of the converted farm buildings to a stile. Over two stiles to cross the corner of a paddock, you descend within the edge of a newly planted copse. Cross a stile and bear half right alongside a paddock.

❺ In the angle of the field go right at a footpath post and cross a footbridge. Soon continue ahead, passing through a hand gate, crossing a footbridge, a stile and another footbridge to a footpath junction. Here cross a stile into the next paddock and bear half left, soon bearing right alongside the hedge. Go through a hedge gap and cross a footbridge to continue ahead in the next field, now on the right hand side of a field.

> ⓘ **EATING AND DRINKING**
> The Coach House in Cowfold is a restaurant and hotel with a village bar. Besides good food they do afternoon teas Monday to Fridays. Along with sandwiches and baguettes, you can get dishes such as sausages and creamy mash, liver and bacon and even moules.

❻ Half-way along the field go right at a footpath post and over a footbridge into a narrow tree belt, mainly coppiced hazel with oak trees. At the end continue ahead, pass a redundant stile onto a lane that leads to the A272. Go left along the pavement towards The Coach House hotel and restaurant. Go right at the roundabout, then left at the next and back to the car park.

*Opposite: Cowfold church*

# DEVIL'S DYKE AND THE WORLD'S GRANDEST VIEW

A fine walk with glimpses over the most famous
of all the dry chalk valleys.

Devil's Dyke is a geological quirk, a spectacular, steep-sided downland combe or cleft 300ft (91m) deep and 0.5 miles (800m) long. According to legend, it was dug by the Devil as part of a trench extending to the sea. It's a charming tale but no one knows for sure how it originated, but it was most likely to have been cut by glacial meltwaters when the ground was permanently frozen in the ice age.

Rising to over 600ft (183m), this most famous of beauty spots is also a magnificent viewpoint where the views stretch for miles in all directions. The Clayton Windmills are visible on a clear day, as are Chanctonbury Ring, Haywards Heath and parts of the Ashdown Forest. The artist John Constable described this view as the grandest in the world.

## A Tourist Honeypot

During the Victorian era and in the early part of the 20th century, the place was akin to a bustling theme park with a cable car crossing the valley and a steam railway coming up from Brighton. On Whit Monday 1893 a staggering 30,000 people visited Devil's Dyke. In 1928, HRH the Duke of York dedicated the Dyke Estate for the use of the public forever and in fine weather it can seem just as crowded as it was in Queen Victoria's day. With the car park full and the surrounding downland slopes busy with people simply taking a relaxing stroll in the sunshine, Devil's Dyke assumes the feel of a seaside resort at the height of the season. Hang-gliders swoop silently over the grassy downland like pterodactyls and kite flyers spill from their cars in search of fun and excitement. But don't let the crowds put you off. The views more than make up for the invasion of visitors, and away from the chalk slopes and the car park the walk soon heads for more peaceful surroundings.

Beginning on Summer Down, on the route of the South Downs Way, you drop down gradually to the village of Poynings where there may be time for a welcome pint at the Royal Oak. Rest and relax for as long as you can here because it's a long, steep climb to the Devil's Dyke pub. The last leg of the walk is gentle and relaxing by comparison.

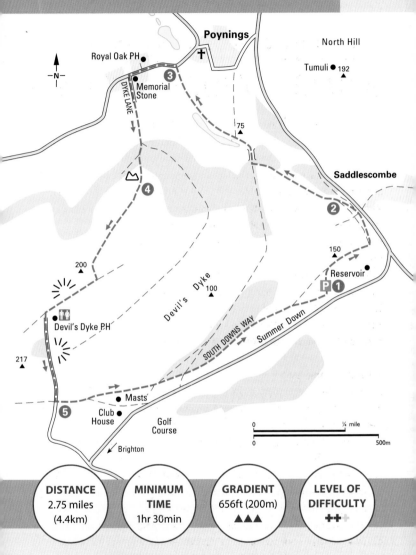

North Hill

Poynings

Royal Oak PH

Tumuli ● 192
▲

**3**

Memorial Stone

DYKE LANE

75

**4**

Saddlescombe

**2**

150
▲

Reservoir

200
▲

Devil's Dyke

P **1**

Devil's Dyke PH

100
▲

SOUTH DOWNS WAY

Summer Down

217
▲

**5**

Masts

Club House

Golf Course

↙ Brighton

0 ——————— ¼ mile
0 ——————— 500m

| DISTANCE | MINIMUM TIME | GRADIENT | LEVEL OF DIFFICULTY |
|---|---|---|---|
| 2.75 miles (4.4km) | 1hr 30min | 656ft (200m) ▲▲▲ | ✚✚✚ |

**PATHS** Field and woodland paths, 7 stiles

**LANDSCAPE** Chalk grassland, steep escarpment and woodland

**SUGGESTED MAP** OS Explorer 122 Brighton & Hove

**START/FINISH** Grid reference: TQ 269112

**DOG FRIENDLINESS** Mostly off lead. On lead on approach to Poynings

**PARKING** Summer Down free car park

**PUBLIC TOILETS** By Devil's Dyke pub

# Walk 20 Devil's Dyke

## WALK 20 DIRECTIONS

**❶** From the Summer Down car park go through the kissing gate and then veer right. Join the South Downs Way and follow it alongside lines of trees. Soon the path curves left and drops down to the road. Part company with the South Downs Way at this point, as it crosses over to join the private road to Saddlescombe Farm, and follow the verge for about 75yds (69m). Bear left at the footpath sign and drop down the bank to a stile.

**❷** Follow the line of the tarmac lane as it curves right to reach a waymark. Leave the lane and walk ahead alongside power lines, keeping the line of trees and bushes on the right. Look for a narrow path disappearing into the vegetation and make for a stile. Drop down some steps into the woods and turn right at a junction with a bridleway. Take the path running off half left and follow it between fields and a wooded dell. Pass over a stile and continue to a stile in the left boundary. Cross a footbridge to a further stile and now turn right towards Poynings.

**❸** Head for a gate and footpath sign and turn left at the road. Follow the parallel path along to the Royal Oak and then continue to Dyke Lane on the left. There is a memorial stone here, dedicated to the memory of George Stephen Cave Cuttress, a resident of Poynings for more than 50 years, and erected by his widow. Follow the tarmac bridleway and soon it narrows to a path. On reaching the fork, by a National Trust sign for Devil's Dyke, veer right and begin climbing the steps.

**❹** Follow the path up to a gate and continue up the steps. From the higher ground there are breathtaking views to the north and west. Make for a kissing gate and head up the slope towards the inn. Keep the Devil's Dyke pub on your left and take the road round to the left, passing a bridleway on the left. Follow the path parallel to the road and look to the left for a definitive view of Devil's Dyke.

**❺** Head for the South Downs Way and turn left by a National Trust sign for Summer Down to a stile and gate. Follow the trail, keeping Devil's Dyke down to your left, and eventually you reach a stile leading into Summer Down car park.

---

### ⓧ EATING AND DRINKING

The Royal Oak located in the centre of Poynings includes a patio and gardens for warm days and offers home-cooked specialities, local seafood, cask ales and summer barbeques. The Devil's Dyke pub, three quarters of the way round the walk, has a family dining area and garden patio. Sunday lunch, baguettes and salads feature on the menu.

# BEEDING'S ROYAL ESCAPE ROUTE

Take a leisurely stroll through the peaceful Adur Valley
to a historic bridge crossed by a fugitive king.

Crossing Beeding Bridge, it is worth stopping for a few moments to consider its importance as a river crossing. Not only does the bridge play a vital part in this walk, allowing you to cross the River Adur easily from one bank to the other, but 360 years ago, in October 1651, it enabled Charles II, defeated and on the run, to escape his enemies and eventually flee to safety in France.

His route through the Adur Valley was one step on a long and eventful journey that has became an integral part of British history. Following the Battle of Worcester, where his army was soundly beaten, the young Charles fled across England, pursued by Parliamentary forces under Oliver Cromwell.

First, he made his way north, intending to cross the River Severn into Wales where he could find a ship and sail to the continent. But the river was heavily guarded and Charles was forced to change his plans.

## Troopers on the Bridge

Instead he travelled south, eventually reaching Charmouth on the Dorset coast. Once again his plans to escape by boat fell through and, in a desperate attempt to avoid capture, he made his way along the south coast to Shoreham near Brighton, where at last he found a ship which could take him to France. His journey through England lasted six weeks and he was loyally supported by his followers, many at great risk to their own lives.

The King's arrival in Bramber was one heart-stopping moment among many during his time on the run. As he and his escort came into the village from the west, they were horrified to find many troopers in the vicinity of the river bank. Charles realised they had been posted here to guard Beeding Bridge, which was his only means of easily reaching Shoreham. Cautiously, he crossed the bridge and continued on his way undetected. Moments later, the Royal party looked round to see a group of cavalry hotly pursuing them across country. Charles feared the worst, but as they reached him, the soldiers suddenly overtook the King and rode off into the distance in the pursuit of someone else. After their narrow escape in the Adur Valley, the group decided it was safer to split up and make their own way to the coast.

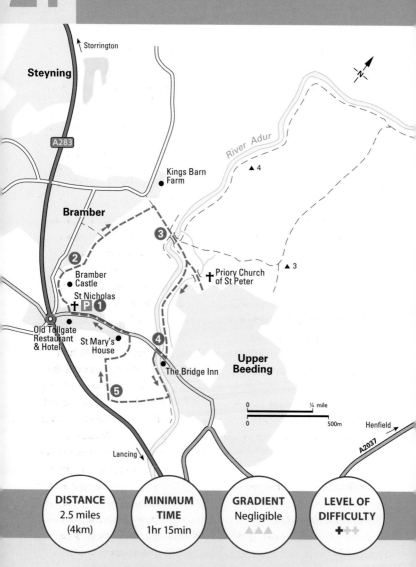

## DISTANCE
2.5 miles
(4km)

## MINIMUM TIME
1hr 15min

## GRADIENT
Negligible

## LEVEL OF DIFFICULTY

**PATHS** Riverside, field and village paths, some road, 10 stiles

**LANDSCAPE** Adur Valley flood plain

**SUGGESTED MAP** OS Explorer 122 Brighton & Hove

**START/FINISH** Grid reference: TQ 185105

**DOG FRIENDLINESS** Take care on approach to Beeding Bridge and in Bramber

**PARKING** Free car park at Bramber Castle

**PUBLIC TOILETS** Bramber and Beeding

## WALK 21 DIRECTIONS

❶ Facing the castle and wooded ramparts, locate the narrow path in the left-hand corner of the parking area and follow it left as it meanders through the trees to the left of the castle ramparts. Keep right up the slope at a fork, then bear left downhill at the next fork to reach a track.

❷ Turn right and head up through the trees, passing gates on the left and right. Continue ahead at the next signpost and the River Adur can be glimpsed between the trees on the right. Pass a footpath on the left and make for a stile ahead. Follow the path to the next stile and footpath sign. Cross over and turn right towards the footbridge spanning the River Adur.

❸ Cross the stile and bridge. Bear right, following the river bank towards Upper Beeding. Branch off left to a footbridge and stile in order to visit the Priory Church of St Peter. Returning to the main walk, continue towards Upper Beeding. Cross a stile by a gate and continue to a kissing gate. Follow the path to the Bridge Inn at Beeding and cross the Adur.

> ### 🌿 ON THE WALK
> Overlooking the Adur Valley and just off the walk is Sele Priory established by William de Braose. Sele is another name for Beeding. The vicarage now occupies the site of the old priory, part of an ancient Benedictine foundation, and next to it is the Priory Church of St Peter.

❹ Swing left and join the right-hand bank, heading downstream. Cross a stile and follow the riverside path. Continue to a right-hand stile and enter the field. Keep the fence on the right and at the fence corner go straight on, out across the field.

❺ As you approach the A283, turn right in front of the stile, towards the trees, with the ruins of Bramber Castle peeping through. Make for a stile and bear right. Follow the track as it bends left and crosses two stiles before joining a tarmac drive running through the trees to the road. Turn left, pass St Mary's House and walk along the High Street, passing the Castle Inn Hotel. At the Old Tollgate Restaurant and hotel, cross the road and follow the steps up to the church and car park.

> ### 🌿 IN THE AREA
> Before starting the walk, have a look at the ruins of Bramber Castle. Now in the care of English Heritage and the National Trust, it was built just after the Norman Conquest to defend the exposed and vulnerable Sussex coast. Next to Bramber Castle is the Parish Church of St Nicholas, originally the castle chapel. Towards the end of the walk, you pass the entrance to St Mary's House in Bramber. This medieval building is one of the best example of late 15th-century timber framing in Sussex.

# STEYNING'S HISTORIC STREETS

Once a river port, stroll through Steyning's rich history and visit one of Sussex's finest parish churches.

The clock tower on the old market house is a reminder that until 1771 there was a timber-framed market house in the middle of the High Street towards the Church Street junction. A market town probably since the 11th century the tolls were claimed by the Abbey of Fecamp in Normandy who then held the church and the manor; consequently controlled Steyning and its market.

Steyning's Norman parish church with the nave arcade columns and arches richly carved with chevron was once much larger. An Anglo-Saxon minster, it was rebuilt by Fecamp Abbey but its transepts, crossing and choir were demolished in the 16th century and only the truncated nave remains, the decaying chancel being described in 1602 as 'a common haunt for pigeons'.

Although endowed in 1614 by William Holland, a local boy made good, the grammar school in Church Street is actually much older. Holland took over the old 15th-century guildhall of the Medieval Fraternity (brotherhood as it says over the door) of the Holy Trinity that had been dissolved by Henry VIII. With a brick porch erected in 1614, the school is one of the best buildings in Church Street.

### A Victorian Scandal

On 26th June 1891, Katharine O'Shea married Charles Stewart Parnell in a house in Church Street. A plaque commemorates this conclusion to a colossal scandal. It was a short marriage as Parnell, his health ruined and his political career as leader of the Irish MPs at Westminster in ruins, died in October, a mere four months later. They had been lovers since the early 1880s and, scandalously, lived together from 1886 but Katharine was still married. Her husband even challenged Parnell to a duel in 1881. Adultery was in those days a very serious matter and of course a mortal sin to a scandalised Irish society. She was nicknamed 'Kitty' by the press and her detractors, a perfectly reasonable diminutive but also in those days slang for a prostitute. Parnell had been forced to resign as leader of the Irish MPs after Katharine's husband had sued for divorce in 1889. The scandal kept the Victorian tabloid press equivalents fully occupied, as of course it would today.

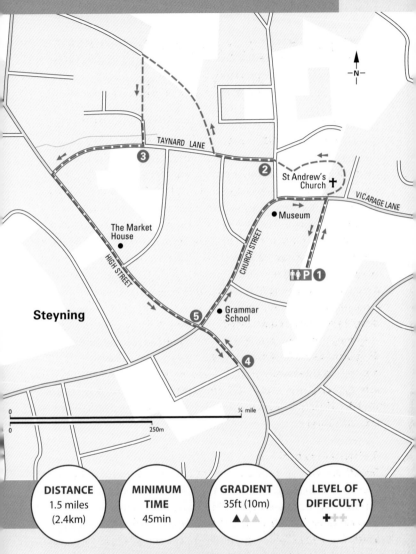

**Steyning**

| DISTANCE | MINIMUM TIME | GRADIENT | LEVEL OF DIFFICULTY |
|---|---|---|---|
| 1.5 miles (2.4km) | 45min | 35ft (10m) ▲▲▲ | ✚✚✚ |

**PATHS** Town roads and footpaths, no stiles

**LANDSCAPE** Historic townscape, curving streets on gentle slopes

**SUGGESTED MAP** OS Explorer 122 Brighton & Hove

**START/FINISH** Grid reference: TQ 178112

**DOG FRIENDLINESS** On lead in the town

**PARKING** Steyning Centre Car Park, accessed from Vicarage Lane

**PUBLIC TOILETS** In the Steyning Centre adjoining the car park

## WALK 22 DIRECTIONS

❶ From the car park head towards Steyning's Norman church, passing a statue of St Cuthman. Visit the church and leaving it go to its right, staying in the churchyard, and pass behind the chancel. As you walk along the path behind the church look to your right at Gatewick House, a good Georgian brick house behind a folly gateway. Reaching a path junction bear right to leave the churchyard.

❷ Continue ahead along Tanyard Lane, going right at a footpath sign just before the 'Stone Croft' sign. Follow the footpath, skirting to the right of The Hollow, bearing left after a cul de sac loop. At a lane go left onto a footpath and continue ahead to a road and towards Steyning Health Centre.

❸ Over a stream bear right, back in Tanyard Lane. At the High Street turn left to gently ascend as the street curves elegantly uphill, passing numerous coffee shops, cafés, tea rooms and pubs. You pass a strange clock turret perching on the gable of a modest tile-hung building. Pass the Church Street junction roundabout and

> ### 🍴 EATING AND DRINKING
> There are numerous cafés, coffee shops and tea rooms in the High Street before you reach the Church Street roundabout. For a pub in the same part of town there is the Chequer Inn, a medieval building with a painted brick Georgian façade.

descend the footpath with pebbled margins on the right side of the road, with a wall between you and the road, still in High Street.

❹ Reaching the pair of preserved 19th-century parish pumps, and a horse drinking trough, cross the road and retrace your steps to the Church Street mini-roundabout.

❺ Turn right to walk down Church Street, the prettiest road in the town, with a concentration of timber-framed houses. Pass No 2 where Charles Stewart Parnell, Irish MP, married Kitty O'Shea in 1891, and the Grammar School founded in 1614. Beyond the library car park turn right at the sign to Steyning Centre and Recycling Point to return to the car park.

> ### 🌿 IN THE AREA
> The lane south from Steyning, on the west side of the Adur, winds along at the foot of the chalk downs with two small, simple country churches, Botolphs and Coombes, the latter in an idyllic location. Continue and you see Lancing College Chapel on its bluff overlooking Shoreham. Towering Victorian Gothic, It was started in 1868 but not finished until 1911. Open every day from 10am to 6pm, it has a stained-glass window dedicated by Archbishop Desmond Tutu in 2007.

# THE DEVIL'S RING

Enjoy a breezy stroll amid ancient history
with fine long views over the Downs to the sea.

Cissbury Ring is credited in legend as the work of the Devil, for when he
was digging the Devil's Dyke near Brighton it is said clods of earth flew from
his presumably gigantic spade and created many of the most prominent
earthworks in Sussex, including Chanctonbury Ring near Washington, Mount
Caburn near Lewes and of course Cissbury Ring. Other past explanations
associate the Ring with Julius Caesar, presumably a fanciful 17th-century
attempt to explain the name as 'Caesar's bury'.

## Men of Flint

Long before the fort appeared the hill had been a major flint mining area.
This was in neolithic times when the pits with their complexes of radiating
galleries were hand excavated using mainly red deer antler picks with their
shoulder blades used as shovels. The seams were about 40ft (12m) below
the surface and this industrial-scale mining took place over 5,000 years ago,
millennia before Iron Age man made his mark. The filled-in shafts and waste
tips can be seen all over the west part of the hill.

## Men of Iron

The hilltop was fortified during the Middle Iron Age, say around 250BC, and
the great rampart and outer ditch enclose a vast 60 acres (24ha). The ditches
have silted up and were originally at least 5ft (1.5m) deeper than now and
the rampart has similarly eroded in height. Also in your mind's eye you must
add timber palisades along the top of the ramparts and so the defences must
have been even more impressive than they seem nowadays. On this route you
enter and leave by the two original now unfortified entrances.

The western half of the ramparts enclose most of the old flint mines, with
a few mines and many spoil heaps outside. The area enclosed by the fort was
large enough for cultivation as well as occupation.

Now owned by the National Trust and, unsurprisingly, a Scheduled Ancient
Monument, it is an enjoyable addition to this walk to stroll along the ramparts
that are about 1 mile (1.6km) in circumference.

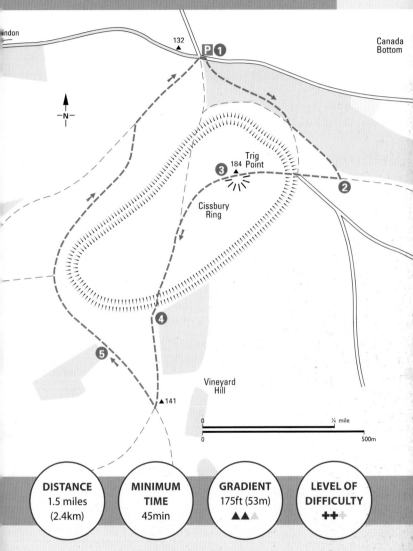

| DISTANCE | MINIMUM TIME | GRADIENT | LEVEL OF DIFFICULTY |
|---|---|---|---|
| 1.5 miles (2.4km) | 45min | 175ft (53m) ▲▲▲ | ++ |

**PATHS** Footpaths, no stiles
**LANDSCAPE** Iron Age hill-fort and chalk hills of the South Downs
**SUGGESTED MAP** OS Explorer 121 Arundel & Pulborough
**START/FINISH** Grid reference: TQ 139085
**DOG FRIENDLINESS** On lead if sheep are grazing the Ring's slopes
**PARKING** Cissbury Ring Car Park, accessed from Findon village centre
**PUBLIC TOILETS** None on route

*Opposite: The Iron Age hill-fort of Cissbury Ring*

**WALK 23 DIRECTIONS**

❶ From the car park cross to a hand gate. Through this bear half left onto a track that skirts to the left of Cissbury Ring, hawks wheeling above. Climb steadily until you reach a gate.

❷ Go through it and bear sharp right alongside a post and wire fence. Cross to the kissing gate ahead. Through this gate, continue ahead, across the hill fort's ring ditch to pass through the gap in the ramparts, the original east gateway, and into the enclosure. Head to the trig point at the hill summit that is 603ft (184m) above sea level.

❸ There are fine views from here over Worthing, well out to sea and a long way along the coast, eastwards to Shoreham with its power station chimney visible and to the west to Littlehampton's gasholder. On a clear day you can see Chichester Cathedral's spire and even the Isle of Wight. Leaving the summit, head generally towards a distant communications mast, the path soon becoming a broad greensward path bearing left towards a clump of trees. This path goes between the trees, mostly oak, ash and sycamore, and leaves Cissbury Ring via the south 'gate' or gap in the rampart and ditch.

❹ Out through a kissing gate follow the path ahead and downhill, woods to your left. At the corner of the wood bear right at a footpath post and follow the path to a hand gate.

❺ Through this gate continue ahead, the path generally keeping parallel to the curve of the ramparts and ditch above to your right and amid downland grass. The path then descends and ascends again briefly, having merged with a track coming in from the left alongside a post and wire fence. Pass through a gate and keep ahead to the gate at the car park.

---

### ✿ IN THE AREA

On the other side of the Findon Valley why not visit High Salvington Windmill (open on the first and third Sundays of each month from April to September and with light refreshments). This is a post mill in which most of the structure rotates to bring the sails to the wind. Built about 1750, it closed in 1897 but had a second life as a tea room! Restored, it now can again grind corn.

---

### 🍴 EATING AND DRINKING

Obviously there is nothing at Cissbury Ring out on the Downs, but there are two pubs in Findon where the lane to the car park begins. One is the Village House that prides itself on its food, both meals and bar snacks, using as much local produce as possible. Adjacent is the other, The Gun Inn, now under new management.

# WHERE COUNTRYSIDE MEETS COAST

The last surviving stretch of undeveloped coast between Bognor Regis and Brighton forms the backdrop to this fascinating walk.

Much of the Sussex coast has grown and evolved since early pioneering photographers captured classic seaside scenes at Worthing, Hove and Littlehampton, and now a chain of urban development extends almost continuously from Bognor to Brighton. Here and there are still hints of the coastline as it used to be before the builders moved in, but Climping Beach, where this walk begins, is an altogether different place. There is a welcome feeling of space and distance here, rarely experienced on the Sussex coast.

**Remote Spot**

One of Climping's main attractions is its remoteness. It is approached along a country lane which terminates at the beach car park. A glance at a map of this area might cause some confusion. The village of Climping, which has a 13th-century church, lies a mile (1.6km) or so inland and the nearest settlement to Climping Beach is Atherington. The medieval church and various dwellings of this old parish now lie beneath the sea, which has steadily encroached upon the land, and all that is now left of low-lying Atherington are several houses and a hotel.

Climping Beach, together with neighbouring West Beach, is popular with holidaymakers as well as locals who want to enjoy the space. The National Trust protects more than 2 miles (3.2km) of coastline here. The low-water, sandy beach is backed by shingle banks which, in places, support vegetation, a rare habitat in Britain. In addition, there are active sand dunes, which are another rare and fragile feature of the coastline. Only six areas of active sand dunes survive on the south coast between Cornwall and Kent and three of them are in Sussex.

After crossing a broad expanse of flat farmland, the walk eventually reaches the River Arun, opposite Littlehampton. From here it's a pleasant amble to West Beach, finishing with a spectacular stroll by the sea, back to Climping Beach. There is much to divert the attention along the way, but it is this lonely stretch of coastline that makes the greatest impression – a vivid reminder of how the entire West Sussex coast once looked.

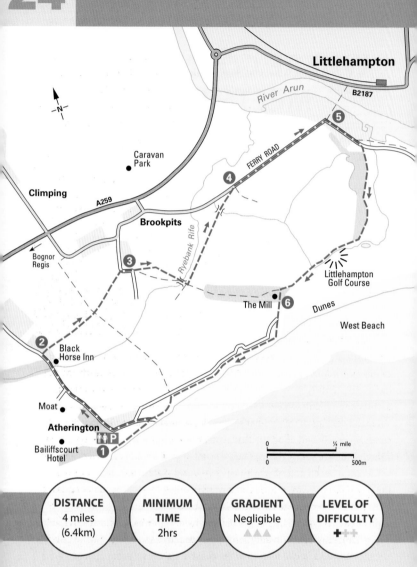

| DISTANCE | MINIMUM TIME | GRADIENT | LEVEL OF DIFFICULTY |
|----------|--------------|----------|---------------------|
| 4 miles (6.4km) | 2hrs | Negligible ▲▲▲ | ✚✚✚ |

**PATHS** Field paths, roads and stretches of beach, 1 stile
**LANDSCAPE** Sandy beaches, open farmland and riverside development
**SUGGESTED MAP** OS Explorer 121 Arundel & Pulborough
**START/FINISH** Grid reference: TQ 005007
**DOG FRIENDLINESS** Off lead on enclosed paths and beach area. Under control
near the Arun and on road at Climping **PARKING** Car park at Climping Beach
**PUBLIC TOILETS** Climping Beach

**WALK 24 DIRECTIONS**

❶ From the beach car park take the road leading away from the sea, passing the entrance to Bailiffscourt Hotel on the left. Roger de Montgomery permitted Benedictine monks from the Abbey of Seez to establish a chapel at Climping. Their bailiff occupied what is now the Bailiffscourt Hotel . The building was later remodelled in the medieval style. Continue along the road until you reach the Black Horse Inn and take the next footpath on the right, by some thatched cottages.

❷ When the track swings left, continue ahead across the field to a signpost, in line with a distant blue building, at a junction with a byway. Go straight over and follow the path through the fields.

❸ By some derelict outbuildings, join a track on a bend and turn right. As it swings right, take the signposted path and begin by following the boundary hedge. Stride out across the field, cross the concrete footbridge and bear left at the footpath sign to follow a deep ditch known as the Ryebank Rife. When the path veers away from the ditch, cross the field to a line of trees, aiming towards a distant blue storage tower. There is a stile to cross here, followed by a footbridge.

❹ Turn right and walk along the road to a turning on the right for Littlehampton Golf Club. The walk follows this road, but before taking it,

continue ahead for a few steps to have a look at the footbridge crossing the Arun. The buildings of Littlehampton can be seen on the far side and, if time allows, you may like to extend the walk by visiting the town.

> 🍴 **EATING AND DRINKING**
>
> The Black Horse Inn near Climping Beach is located on the route of the walk and is an ideal stop if you're completing it on a summer's evening. Eat and drink outside or relax in the cosy bar. The inn offers a range of ales and a wide selection of hot and cold food. Littlehampton has a good choice of pubs, including several in the vicinity of the Arun.

❺ Continuing the main walk, follow the road towards West Beach and the golf club, veering right at a car park sign to follow an enclosed path to a kissing gate and briefly cross the golf course to enter a wood. The path runs along a raised bank and later emerges into the open with good views over this unspoilt coastal plain. Keep to the path and at the end of the golf course you reach a house known as The Mill. Avoid the path on the right here and keep left.

❻ Continue walking along the footpath and soon it reaches West Beach. Look for the interpretation board. Follow the footpath sign towards Climping, skirting the edge of the beach and avoiding a byway on the right as you approach the car park.

# STANDING GUARD OVER ARUNDEL

A varied walk following the River Arun to Arundel Park and concluding with a tour of this handsome Sussex town.

There has been a castle here since the 11th century, though most of the present fortification is Victorian. Arundel Castle is the principal ancestral home of the Dukes of Norfolk, formerly the Earls of Arundel, and the family have lived at Arundel since the 16th century.

The castle was attacked by Parliamentary forces during the Civil War. However, it was rebuilt and restored in the 18th and 19th centuries. Within its great walls lies a collection of furniture dating from the 16th century, tapestries, clocks and portraits by Van Dyck, Gainsborough, Reynolds, Mytens and Lawrence – among others. There are also personal items belonging to Mary, Queen of Scots, and religious and heraldic items from the Duke of Norfolk's collection.

### Saving the Best for Last

The walk starts down by the Arun and from here there are teasing glimpses of the castle, but it is not until you have virtually finished the walk that you reach its main entrance. Following the river bank through the tranquil Arun Valley, renowned for its bird life, the walk eventually reaches Arundel Park. Swanbourne Lake, a great attraction for young children, lies by the entrance to the park, making it easily accessible for everyone.

Once the bustling lakeside scene fades from view and the sound of children playing finally fades, however, the park assumes a totally different character. Rolling hills and tree-clad slopes crowd in from every direction and only occasional serious walkers, some of them following the long distance Monarch's Way recreational path, are likely to be seen in these more remote surroundings.

You may feel isolated, briefly cut off the from the rest of the world at this point, but the interlude is soon over when you find yourself back in Arundel. Pass the huge edifice of the cathedral, built in 1870, and make your way down to the castle entrance. Walk down the High Street, said to be the steepest in England, and by the bridge at the bottom you can see the remains of the Blackfriars monastery, dissolved in 1546 by Henry VIII.

*Opposite: The Bevis Tower, Arundel Castle*

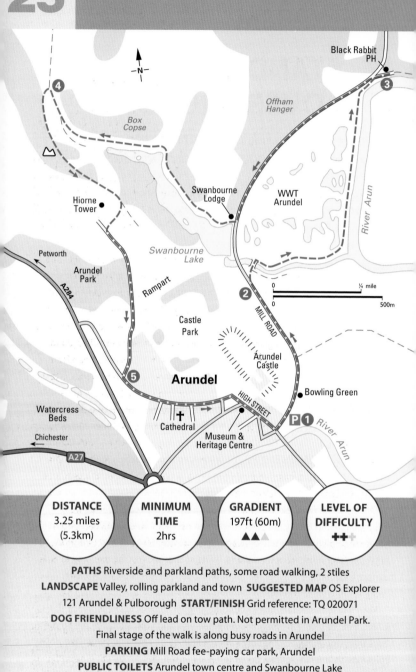

Black Rabbit PH

❸

Offham Hanger

❹

Box Copse

—N—

Swanbourne Lodge

WWT Arundel

River Arun

Hiorne Tower

Swanbourne Lake

0    ¼ mile

0    500m

Petworth

A284

Arundel Park

Rampart

❷

MILL ROAD

Castle Park

Arundel Castle

❺

**Arundel**

HIGH STREET

Bowling Green

P ❶    River Arun

Watercress Beds

✝ Cathedral

Museum & Heritage Centre

Chichester

A27

| DISTANCE | MINIMUM TIME | GRADIENT | LEVEL OF DIFFICULTY |
|---|---|---|---|
| 3.25 miles (5.3km) | 2hrs | 197ft (60m) ▲▲▲ | ✚✚✚ |

**PATHS** Riverside and parkland paths, some road walking, 2 stiles
**LANDSCAPE** Valley, rolling parkland and town  **SUGGESTED MAP** OS Explorer
121 Arundel & Pulborough  **START/FINISH** Grid reference: TQ 020071
**DOG FRIENDLINESS** Off lead on tow path. Not permitted in Arundel Park.
Final stage of the walk is along busy roads in Arundel
**PARKING** Mill Road fee-paying car park, Arundel
**PUBLIC TOILETS** Arundel town centre and Swanbourne Lake
**NOTE** Arundel Park is closed annually on 24 March

## WALK 25 DIRECTIONS

❶ From the car park in Mill Road, turn right and walk along the tree-lined pavement. Pass the bowling green and a glance to your left will reveal a dramatic view of Arundel Castle.

❷ Follow the road to the elegant stone bridge, avoid the first path on the right and cross over via a footbridge and turn right to join the riverside path, partly shaded by overhanging trees. Emerging from the trees, the path cuts across lush, low-lying ground to reach the western bank of the Arun. Turn left here and walk beside the reed-fringed Arun to the Black Rabbit pub, which can be seen standing out against a curtain of trees.

❸ From the Black Rabbit, turn left on the minor road back towards Arundel, passing the entrance to the WWT Arundel Wetland Centre. Make for the gate leading into Arundel Park and follow the path alongside Swanbourne Lake. Eventually the lake fades from view as the walk reaches deeper into the park. Ignore a turning branching off to the left, just before a gate and stile, and follow the path as it curves gently to the right.

### ⚘ ON THE WALK

Climbing up from Arundel Park brings you to Hiorne Tower, a folly. Triangular in plan and recently restored, the folly was built by Francis Hiorne in an effort to ingratiate himself with the then Duke of Norfolk so that he might work on the restoration of Arundel Castle. The Duke agreed but Hiorne died before he could begin work.

❹ Turn sharply to the left at the next waymarked junction and begin a fairly steep ascent, with the footpath through the park seen curving away down to the left, back towards the lake. This stretch of the walk offers glorious views over Arundel Park. Head for a stile and gate, then bear immediately right up the bank. Cross the grass, following the waymarks and keeping to the left of Hiorne Tower. On reaching a driveway, turn left and walk down to Park Lodge. Keep to the right by the private drive and make for the road.

❺ Turn left, pass the cathedral and bear left at the junction by the entrance to the castle. Go down the hill into the centre of Arundel. Mill Road is at the bottom of the High Street.

### 🍴 EATING AND DRINKING

Arundel offers a good choice of places to eat and drink. The Black Rabbit at Offham, on the route of the walk, is delightfully situated on the Arun. Cheerful hanging baskets add plenty of colour in summer when you can sit outside and relax in these very attractive surroundings. The WWT Arundel Wetland Centre offers a café by the water's edge and there is a picnic site by Swanbourne Lake.

# WALKING TO SCOTLAND

A walk through coppice woodland, the rich arable land of the Sussex coastal plain and a visit to two interesting churches

In the south side of the churchyard at Walberton is an enormous pink granite family vault enclosed by railings, a typical piece of Victorian grandiosity and probably built by Richard Prime MP in the 1860s. This is the Prime family's vault, the 19th-century owners of Walberton House, immediately east of the church and now renamed Walberton Park.

The present stuccoed house replaced an old 17th-century manor house and its short-lived successor. General John Whyte bought the estate in 1801 and had the 17th-century mansion pulled down to be replaced by one of his own design. Presumably a better general than an architect, the next owner Richard Prime had to demolish it in 1817 because it was so badly built.

This time a proper architect was employed, no less than Sir Robert Smirke whose notable buildings include Eastnor Castle in Herefordshire and the British Museum. Sadly it suffered various reductions and partial demolitions in the 20th century, but is now safe and converted into apartments.

## Binsted

Within the copses on the northern section of this walk the wide track has well defined banks on each side as it passes through Singer's Piece and Scotland. It is thought this was the course of the old Roman road to Chichester and was mentioned in 13th- and 14th-century documents as a 'king's highway'. Still shown as a road on 17th-century maps, it was called Arundel Highway in 1727, then Scotland Lane. Scotland has nothing to do with the country, it simply relates to the customary or scot rent system once in use here.

This section of the route, within the coppices, is within the boundaries of the relatively new South Downs National Park.

Binsted church is isolated on its lane, the village having shrivelled away to a couple of farmhouses and The Black Horse pub. The church is mainly Norman and a delightful rural one with three Norman windows surviving, including one with 12th-century wall painting in the splays. The font is also Norman, a bulbous bowl with an arcade decoration.

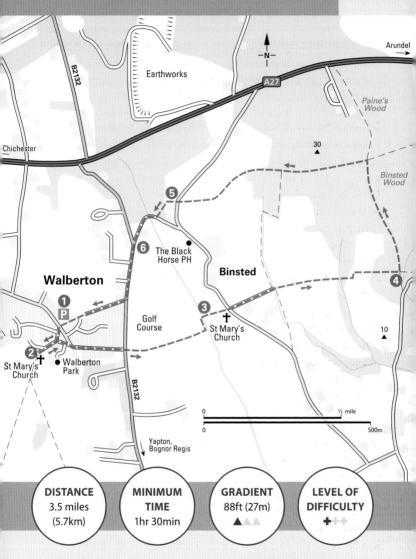

## DISTANCE
3.5 miles
(5.7km)

## MINIMUM TIME
1hr 30min

## GRADIENT
88ft (27m)
▲▲▲

## LEVEL OF DIFFICULTY
✚✚✚

**PATHS** Field paths, woodland paths and track and village pavements, 1 stile
**LANDSCAPE** Mainly arable fields and coppiced woodland
**SUGGESTED MAP** OS Explorer 121 Arundel & Pulborough
**START/FINISH** Grid reference: SU 972059
**DOG FRIENDLINESS** On a lead in Walberton village
**PARKING** Walberton Village Hall Car Park, next to local shops
**PUBLIC TOILETS** None on route

**WALK 26 DIRECTIONS**

❶ From the car park cross the road to the sign for the parish church and continue ahead down Church Lane to the church. From the churchyard you can see Walberton House (now renamed Walberton Park), a restrained stuccoed house by Sir Robert Smirke.

❷ Retrace your steps, bearing right alongside the wall to reach Walberton Park and then continue along the village road, passing an old brewery, formerly Ellis & Sons which closed in the 1920s and is now converted to dwellings with helpful brewery-inspired names. Reaching a mini-roundabout cross the road. Through a kissing gate you leave the village behind, walking between fields. At a kissing gate descend through a golf course to cross over a stream on a footbridge, Binsted church is visible ahead.

❸ At the footpath sign bear right and continue uphill alongside a post and wire fence. At the lane go through a kissing gate and bear right to visit

> **🍴 EATING AND DRINKING**
>
> The Black Horse in Binsted, on the lane Between Binsted church and Point ❺ has a good restaurant and is very popular. The Hollytree Inn in Walberton is also a good option for refreshments or you can get iron rations at the Turnpike Village Stores next to the car park.

Binsted church. Leaving the churchyard cross the lane to follow a track, initially alongside a flint wall, and continue ahead at a footpath junction towards woods. Pass through this woodland belt and bear left, then right alongside the field-edge. Continue ahead into the woods as far as a footpath cross path signpost.

❹ Bear left and follow the clear path north through the woods that are hazel coppices with mainly beech and oak tree standards. At a footpath cross path post, just before a bench, go left along a track and cross a footbridge. Continue ahead, still in the coppice woodland, now with some sweet chestnut, another popular coppice tree. Passing a footpath post, you emerge from the woods, a view of the sea to your left. Continue along this path, once a Roman road that becomes a green lane and then reaches a road.

❺ Bear left onto the lane, then shortly go right over a stile, just before a house. Follow the path beside a flint wall, then alongside a closeboarded fence to reach a footbridge and bear right along the lane that ascends to the main road.

❻ Here bear left and shortly cross to a pavement and follow it as far as a footpath sign and bear right into Avisford Park Lane. Follow this to its end, shortly becoming a footpath and at its end go right to the car park.

*Opposite: Shady Binsted Wood*

# TORTINGTON: CHURCH AND PRIORY

This walk visits a delightful Norman church that has long outlived its medieval owner, Tortington Priory.

Sandwiched between the partly 16th-century and Georgian Manor Farm and greatly enlarged farm buildings to the south, this parish church is one of great charm and interest with a neat white painted timber belfry at the west end. Norman, probably mid-12th century in date, the little church had a south aisle added in the 13th century but thankfully the builders valued the ornately carved Norman south doorway sufficiently highly to re-use it. The aisle itself was rebuilt and a south chapel added to the chancel around 1903, again reusing the Norman doorway.

The chancel arch is of great interest, its arch fringed with the Norman 'beakhead' ornament, each arch stone carved with grotesque bird and animal heads grasping a stone roll. At the top of the arch is a 1750 keystone inserted to prevent the arch collapsing due to the outward tilting walls. The font is also a Norman one, large and cup shaped and decorated with a frieze of arches on columns.

### Tortington Priory

Founded before 1200 as a house of Augustinian canons, the endowment included, not surprisingly, Tortington's parish church. It was never a large priory and often had the dubious distinction of being used as a place of banishment for disobedient canons as well as for the recuperation of monks disabled by illness.

The priory was dissolved in the 1530s, its prior, a retired prior and five canons all receiving pensions. One of the earlier priors was described unflatteringly in a papal bull issued in 1376. The pope wrote 'on account of the evil rule of our beloved son John Palmere (the Prior) – if indeed he ought to be called beloved'.

Of this priory only the north wall of the nave of the church remains with blocked 13th-century windows and vaulting shafts, preserved in a barn while the old fish ponds to the south remain as ornamental ones, much changed. The quality of the 13th-century nave indicates the standard may have been as high as Boxgrove's chancel (see Walk 35).

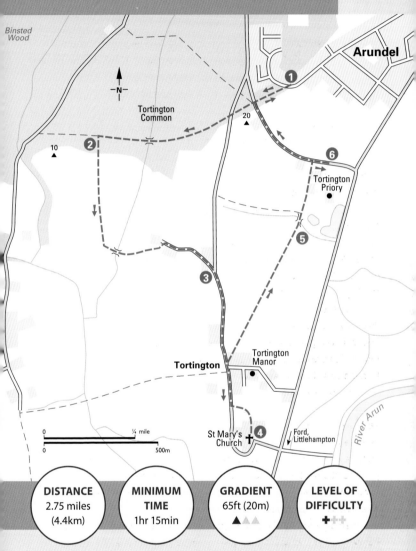

| DISTANCE | MINIMUM TIME | GRADIENT | LEVEL OF DIFFICULTY |
|---|---|---|---|
| 2.75 miles (4.4km) | 1hr 15min | 65ft (20m) ▲▲▲ | ✚✚✚ |

**PATHS** Field and woodland paths, a couple of stretches on country lanes, 2 stiles
**LANDSCAPE** Coppiced woodland on higher ground, pasture and arable on the flatter southern section **SUGGESTED MAP** OS Explorer 121 Arundel & Pulborough
**START/FINISH** Grid reference: TQ 004064
**DOG FRIENDLINESS** On a lead on the country lane parts of the route
**PARKING** In Dallaway Road, accessed from the Ford Road, Arundel
**PUBLIC TOILETS** None on route

## WALK 27 DIRECTIONS

**1** Park at the western end of Dallaway Road, near the footpath post by an electricity substation. Over the stile follow the path through a wood and leave it over a stile at a lane. Cross the lane to continue ahead, still in woodland. Soon reaching another lane cross it and pass a stile to continue ahead, now in hazel coppiced woodland. Cross a stream via a footbridge and, reaching a footpath post, bear left to the edge of the wood.

**2** Out of the wood continue ahead across an arable field. At the trees continue ahead within the tree belt and leave it via a footbridge. Bear left along the field-edge, next going left at a footpath post onto a farm track. Follow this track to a lane.

**3** Bear right past Manor Farm Livery Stables and follow the lane, passing The Arundel Equine Hospital and go half left at a footpath post to cross the lawns of Tortington Manor to another footpath guide post. Here bear right to enter the churchyard of St Mary Magdalene parish church via an iron gate between high gate piers.

**4** After visiting this delightful little Norman church retrace your steps through the gateway and back to the lane. Here bear right along it as far as a pillar box and bear right through a kissing gate. Continue quarter left across grass, again belonging

to the Tortington Manor housing development, to a guidepost, Arundel Castle and Cathedral visible far ahead. Step through a low wall and follow the bearing of the footpath post, generally aiming towards the cathedral.

> ### 🍴 EATING AND DRINKING
> There used to be a pub by Ford Station but that has closed, so beyond the level crossing bear left at sign for the Ship and Anchor. The pub is by the River Arun and does good pub food, including popular Sunday roasts, and real ales.

**5** At the far end of this huge arable field cross a footbridge and immediately bear right over another, then left up what can be a rather nettled path. To your right, but not particularly visible, are the medieval fishponds that supplied carp and other fish to the table of the canons of Tortington Priory. Continue to the road, passing the converted buildings of Priory Farm, now partly renamed 'Brooklands'. At the lane bear right for about 50yds (46m).

**6** Pause here and look right towards a thatched barn. This incorporates on its south wall the remaining part of Tortington Priory, the north wall of the nave. Retrace your steps and continue along the lane past Priory Farm Cottage. Reaching the woods bear right over the stile and through the wood back to the stile at Point **1**.

# TREASURES IN TRUST ON THE SLINDON ESTATE

Tour and explore a sprawling National Trust estate on this glorious woodland walk, which offers fine views of Sussex.

It all began in 1895, the year the National Trust was founded by three far-sighted, visionary Victorians whose objective was to acquire sites of historic interest and natural beauty for the benefit of the nation.

## Slindon Estate

Much of the West Sussex village of Slindon is part of the National Trust's 3,500-acre (1,418ha) Slindon Estate, which is situated on the southern slopes of the South Downs between Arundel and Chichester. The estate, the setting for this walk, was originally designed and developed as an integrated community and it is the Trust's aim to maintain this structure.

Take a stroll through Slindon village as you end the walk and you can see that many of the cottages are built of brick and flint, materials typical of chalk country. During the medieval period, long before the National Trust was established, Slindon was an important estate of the Archbishops of Canterbury. Even earlier it was home to Neolithic people who settled at Barkhale, a hilltop site at its northern end.

## Downland Scenery

As well as the village, the estate consists of a large expanse of sweeping downland dissected by dry valleys, a folly, several farms and a stretch of Roman road. Glorious hanging beechwoods on the scarp enhance the picture, attracting walkers and naturalists in search of peace and solitude. Parts of the estate were damaged in the storms of 1987 and 1990, though the woods are regenerating, with saplings and woodland plants flourishing in the lighter glades. Typical ground plants of the beechwoods include bluebell, dog's mercury, greater butterfly orchid and wood sedge.

To help celebrate its centenary in 1995, the National Trust chose the Slindon Estate to launch its 100 Paths Project, a scheme designed to enhance access to its countryside properties by creating or improving paths. This glorious, unspoiled landscape offers many miles of footpaths and bridleways, making it an excellent choice for a country walk.

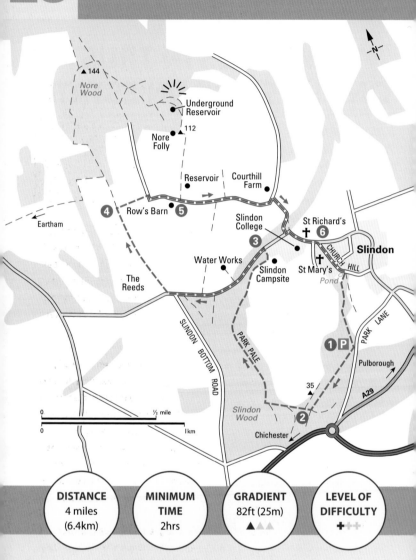

- ▲ 144
- *Nore Wood*
- Underground Reservoir
- ▲ 112
- Nore Folly
- Reservoir
- Courthill Farm
- **4** Row's Barn **5**
- Eartham
- Slindon College
- St Richard's ✝ **6**
- **Slindon**
- **3**
- CHURCH HILL
- Water Works
- Slindon Campsite
- St Mary's ✝
- *Pond*
- The Reeds
- PARK LANE
- SLINDON BOTTOM ROAD
- PARK PALE
- **1** 🅿
- Pulborough
- 35 ▲
- A29
- *Slindon Wood*
- **2**
- Chichester

0 ½ mile
0 1km

| DISTANCE | MINIMUM TIME | GRADIENT | LEVEL OF DIFFICULTY |
|---|---|---|---|
| 4 miles (6.4km) | 2hrs | 82ft (25m) ▲▲▲ | ✚✚✚ |

**PATHS** Woodland, downland paths and tracks, 4 stiles

**LANDSCAPE** Sweeping downland and woodland

**SUGGESTED MAP** OS Explorer 121 Arundel & Pulborough

**START/FINISH** Grid reference: SU 960076

**DOG FRIENDLINESS** Unless signed otherwise, off lead, except in Slindon village

**PARKING** Free National Trust car park in Park Lane, Slindon

**PUBLIC TOILETS** None on route

## WALK 28 DIRECTIONS

❶ From the car park walk towards the road and turn right at a 'No riding' sign, passing through the gate to join a wide straight path cutting between trees and bracken. The path runs alongside sunny glades and clearings and between lines of attractive beech and silver birch trees before reaching a crossroads.

❷ Turn right to a second crossroads and continue ahead here, keeping the grassy bank and ditch, all that remains of the Park Pale, on your right. Follow the broad path as it begins a wide curve to the right and the boundary ditch is still visible here, running parallel to the path. On reaching a kissing gate, keep ahead, soon skirting fields. As you approach the entrance to Slindon campsite, swing left and follow the track down to the road.

### 🍴 EATING AND DRINKING

The George Inn at Eartham (off the route by 0.75 miles/1.2km) has a choice of food, with pasta, pies and rice dishes, as well as steaks. The bar and dining room area are open plan and there is a secluded beer garden.

❸ Turn left and follow the road through the woodland. Pass Slindon Bottom Road and turn right after a few paces to join a bridleway. Follow the path as it cuts between fields and look for a path on the right.

### 🔍 IN THE AREA

Have a look at the Church of St Mary, which is partly Norman and greatly restored. Inside is a rare wooden effigy to Sir Anthony St Leger who died in 1539. Slindon House, now part of a college, was one of the resthouses of the Archbishops of Canterbury during the Middle Ages.

❹ Cross the stile, go down the field, up the other side to the next stile and join a track. Turn right and follow it as it immediately bends left. Walk along to Row's Barn and continue ahead on the track. Nore folly can be seen over to the left.

❺ Continue ahead along the track, following it down to double gates and a stile. Pass to the right of Courthill Farm, turn right and follow the lane or soon branch left on to a parallel woodland path to the next road. Bear left and pass Slindon College on the right and St Richard's Catholic Church on the left before reaching Church Hill.

❻ Fork right into Church Hill, pass the church and make for the pond, a familiar weeping willow reaching down to the water's edge. Look for mallard ducks here. Turn right around the far end of the pond on the waterside path to enter the wood. On reaching a fork, by a National Trust sign for the Slindon Estate, keep left and walk through the trees, to return to the car park.

# THE TOWN AT THE DUKE'S GATES

Enjoy both a fine historic town in the lee of
a major country house and a rich pastoral landscape.

Petworth perches precariously, hemmed in between the walls of Petworth
House's grounds and the deep cut valley to the east of the town. Its streets are
narrow with sharp corners and it has been and remains a traffic bottleneck.

In the 1970s, Petworth was threatened with a north–south bypass but
a vigorous campaign assisted by writers like Marcus Binney fortunately
succeeded in stopping the bypass (for the moment) but of course the traffic
has not gone away.

Lombard Street is the prettiest in the town and traffic free, while East Street
has perhaps the grandest town houses. The area around the market square
has many timber-framed buildings and the town has numerous antiques
shops. In the centre is the Town Hall, a two storey stone building with arched
windows built in 1793 made rather special by the superb bust of William III
added on the north wall that looks French late 17th century and probably
carved during the King's lifetime. Perhaps it was sculpted by Prost of Dijon, the
designer of the amazing (and very French Baroque) trophies of armour atop
Petworth House's great gate piers.

## Petworth Church

The church tower is a bit dissappointing. Stone in the lower stages, the upper
part is 1827 brick, originally rendered, and above it was a spire more suited to
a suburban church in Ealing. Apparently Sir Charles Barry used a design he was
preparing for a church in Brighton. The spire was taken down in 1947 and the
present parapet and shallow tiled pyramidal roof was built in 1953.

## The Cottages of Byworth

The route also passes through Byworth, a small village poised above the east
bank of the deep cut stream. Apart from a pub, The Black Horse that has a tall
brick block and a 16th-century rear, there are two attractive and much painted
cottages where the walk turns left off the main street. Both have whitewashed
infill panels to their timber framing and are jettied, the upper storey projecting
on curved brackets beyond the ground floor.

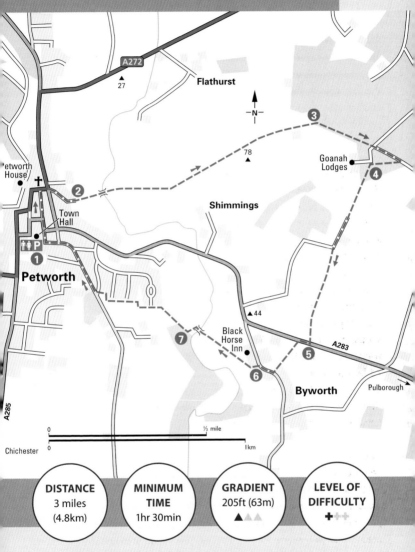

| DISTANCE | MINIMUM TIME | GRADIENT | LEVEL OF DIFFICULTY |
|----------|--------------|----------|---------------------|
| 3 miles (4.8km) | 1hr 30min | 205ft (63m) ▲▲▲ | ✚✚✚ |

**PATHS** Field paths and tracks, pavements in Petworth, 8 stiles

**LANDSCAPE** Rolling, pastoral countryside, woodland and a historic townscape

**SUGGESTED MAP** OS Explorer 133 Haslemere & Petersfield

**START/FINISH** Grid reference: SU 975215

**DOG FRIENDLINESS** On a lead through the horse and cattle pasture on the northern section of the walk and on lead in town

**PARKING** Car park in the centre of Petworth **PUBLIC TOILETS** In the car park

## WALK 29 DIRECTIONS

❶ Leave the car park via the Old Bakery Shopping Arcade. Continue towards the church tower. Pass the Town Hall and continue up Lombard Street. At the top bear right towards Sir Charles Barry's 1851 Gothic lamp standard and cross East Street into Bartons Lane. Follow this, bearing left and becoming a footpath, to a kissing gate.

❷ Through the kissing gate there is a splendid view across the valley and a rolling pastoral landscape, unbelievably, once threatened with a bypass. Descend to a stone bridge, over it continuing ahead to a hedge corner. Reaching this continue ahead alongside the hedge. Over a stile, now on the Serpent's Trail way marked route, and at the hedge corner, bear half left to pass between two conifer clumps.

❸ Descend to a stile by an oak tree and over this ascend between hedges. At the top bear half right and continue on the track along the edge of and then within woodland. Continue ahead across several cross tracks and where

the path meets a metalled track bear sharp right along it towards a pair of large stone Petworth Estate gate piers with the Goanah Lodges.

❹ Just before the gate piers bear left onto a track passing a reservoir and follow this through a field gate and out of the woods. Descend past farm buildings and cross a stile. Continue to cross a large field to a stile by the road.

❺ Cross the road and bear right to a stile across the road. Over this follow a post and wire fence to the far corner of the field. Cross a stile and descend to a field gate. Through this turn right on the lane through Byworth village.

❻ Go left at a telephone box onto a tarmac lane, then through a gate ahead. Follow a path that bears right to a footbridge, a pond to your left, and cross a stile. Now in a paddock, go left alongside a fence and at the far end climb a stile and bear left down to a footbridge over a stream.

❼ Over the footbridge bear right and climb, continuing through a kissing gate. At a path fork bear left and climb a field. At the crest keep ahead, garden fences and hedges to your right, a post and wire fence and paddocks to your left. Reaching the road bear right and follow it, eventually curving left and becoming the High Street, into the town centre. At the Oakapple shop bear left back to the car park.

---

### 🍽 EATING AND DRINKING

If you continue a little further along Byworth's main street The Black Horse Inn is an excellent country pub with a restaurant. In Petworth there is a lot of choice, including, besides pubs, the Coco Café and Sugar Lounge in Saddlers Row.

---

# A COMMON INHERITANCE

Stroll through centuries of fascinating landscape history now being restored by the enterprising Sussex Wildlife Trust.

In 1980 the Sussex Wildlife trust bought 185 acres (75ha) of Ebernoe Common whose woodland was under threat. Now owning a larger acreage, much of it a Site of Special Scientific Interest (SSSI), the Trust has a very carefully thought out management plan to restore the common back to wood pasture and restore the glades that were once so characteristic of the area. You can see ancient oaks and beech trees, clearings, coppicing and much more besides. Ebernoe Common is rich in species with, for example, over 900 species of fungi and 375 species of wild flowers and grasses.

The cattle grids crossed on this route are to keep the cattle in. These have been introduced to restore much of the wood pasture character of the common. The aim is to graze away the coarse undergrowth of past neglect and you will probably see the attractive Sussex cattle hard at work.

**The Common**
By the 14th century the common was mainly used as pig pasture but it was also used for timber and firewood collection. From the late 16th century industry arrived with an iron furnace, its waterwheel-driven furnace bellows and trip hammer powered by water from Furnace Pond, the furnace fed by locally coppiced wood. The pond dammed a stream and you walk along the dam and cross the pond on a footbridge.

The route passes a brick kiln that has recently been restored as part of the common's improvement programme. First shown on an estate map in 1764, the kiln functioned until the 1930s and, not surprisingly, it made the bricks for Ebernoe church in the 1860s.

Ebernoe parish was carved out of nearby Kirdford parish in 1874, the impetus having come from the building of a chapel of ease here in the 1860s. It is built in red brick with bands of yellow and black brick, a Victorian style known rather grandly as 'constructional polychromy'. Inside, by contrast, the church is whitewashed and simple. The lord of the manor, W R Peachey paid the £1,200 building costs and the churchyard wall was built in brick mainly to keep out the common's rabbits.

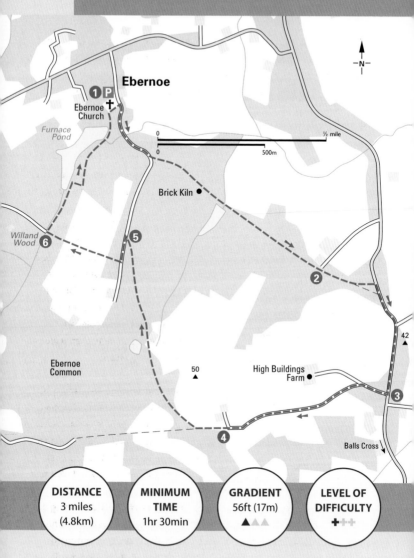

**Ebernoe**

**①** **P**

Ebernoe
Church

*Furnace
Pond*

Brick Kiln ●

—N—

*Willand
Wood* **⑥**

**⑤**

**②**

42
▲

Ebernoe
Common

50
▲

High Buildings
Farm ●

**③**

**④**

Balls Cross

0 ─ ½ mile
0 ─ 500m

---

| DISTANCE | MINIMUM TIME | GRADIENT | LEVEL OF DIFFICULTY |
|---|---|---|---|
| 3 miles (4.8km) | 1hr 30min | 56ft (17m) ▲▲▲ | ✚✚✚ |

**PATHS** Woodland paths and tracks, field paths and tracks, 1 stile

**LANDSCAPE** Heath and wood and former iron industry hammer ponds

**SUGGESTED MAP** OS Explorer 133 Haslemere & Petersfield

**START/FINISH** Grid reference: SU 975272

**DOG FRIENDLINESS** Cattle have been introduced to graze part of the common

**PARKING** Car Park by Ebernoe parish church

**PUBLIC TOILETS** None on route

## WALK 30 DIRECTIONS

**❶** From the car park head down the track to the left of the churchyard and a Sussex Wildlife Trust sign. Continue along the track, passing through a gate beside a cattle grid to continue ahead (not right), through old hazel coppicing amid the oak, beech and ash trees. You pass a brick kiln, a Scheduled Ancient Monument, and cross a causeway between ponds. The path ascends again, before levelling and continues to a gate by another cattle grid. Through this continue on the path and emerge from the wooded common.

> ### 🍴 EATING AND DRINKING
> If you carried on along the lane from Point ❸ for 500yds (457m) you reach Balls Cross and The Stag Inn, the nearest pub to the walk route. It is well known for its local atmosphere, stone flagged floors and traditional country food, including game in season.

**❷** Continue across the grass, a cottage with a large pond in its garden to your left. Bear half left along the edge of the woods, still on a wide grass strip. Where the hedge goes left continue ahead into the wood and wind through the wood over a footbridge, then half left to a road. Bear right along the lane as far as a footpath sign on the right.

**❸** Here bear right along a track, taking the left fork at a footpath signpost beside an old oak tree. Continue along this track between trim hedges, diverting briefly at a kissing gate to read about the Butcherland Fields restoration project on an information board. Back on the track continue to the crest.

**❹** Continue with High Buildings Farm to your right, the common to your left. Still on the track, a hedge on your right, continue past a few footpath posts and where the track bears quarter right continue ahead into the wooded common at a footpath post. Follow the path and bear half right at a footpath post and cross a footbridge. Continue to another footbridge across a pond outlet. Pass through a bridlegate and follow the clear path, eventually converging with a track.

**❺** Pass between three posts and bear left along the track as far as a footpath sign where you bear right along a track to a bridle gate. Through the gate, you cross a field alongside a hedge. Pass a stile and descend into Willand Wood.

**❻** Just before a footbridge bear right and follow the winding path roughly parallel to a stream. The path climbs right and bears left at a Sussex Wildlife Trust post and continues to the banks of a large hammer pond, Furnace Pond. Cross the footbridge over the outlet weir and bear left, still alongside the pond, and climb steps out of the valley. At the top bear half right to the church and the end of the walk.

# PRIORY AND COMMONS

Walk through beautiful scenery with coppiced woods, common heath and a Golden Valley, to pass a moated priory.

Linchmere and the Golden Valley really has some gorgeous scenery. At the northern borders of Sussex the area feels intimate with its heavily wooded and secluded nature. The walk passes through sweet chestnut coppices and across a common managed by the Lynchmere Society through, among other measures, scrub and bracken clearance, cattle grazing and hazel coppicing.

## Shulbrede Priory: Another Lost Priory

Sussex seems unusually rich in the remnants of small abbeys and priories and Linchmere parish has a fine example of the type. From the road Shulbrede Priory looks like a fairly normal 16th- or 17th-century stone house, but it is in fact part of the medieval prior's lodging and of the canon's refectory or dining hall, and mainly 13th century in date. Within the courtyard that occupies some of the priory's lost cloisters is an elegant arcade with trefoil arches that was part of the *lavatorium*, the canon's wash house.

Besides the medieval remains there was a significant addition made after the priory was suppressed and became an Elizabethan house. A medieval partition inserted in the prior's hall above the undercroft was painted with figures of birds and animals declaring the Nativity of Jesus, ladies in Elizabethan costume and even a building that probably represents the priory. In the 17th century the arms of James I were added.

## A Timber Belfry in Stone: Linchmere Church

From the outside, it has to be written, Linchmere's parish church of St Peter looks fairly routine. However a dinky little 13th-century belfry tower was added to a Norman nave and when you go inside you see the round-headed Norman west doorway arch, now leading into a western vestry. Next to this, though are the supports for the east wall of the tower, an arcade of three mid 13th-century arches carried on very tall slender columns. It is as if the belfry, of the dimensions of the more usual timber one, has been petrified and the supporting posts also transformed into stone. Inside, these columns are an unexpected sight and give this little church a surprisingly monumental scale.

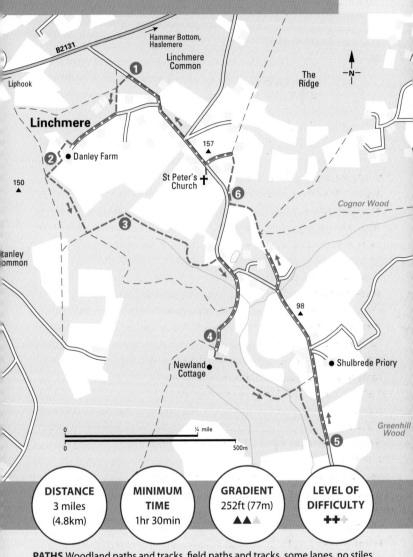

| DISTANCE | MINIMUM TIME | GRADIENT | LEVEL OF DIFFICULTY |
|---|---|---|---|
| 3 miles (4.8km) | 1hr 30min | 252ft (77m) ▲▲▲ | ++✛ |

**PATHS** Woodland paths and tracks, field paths and tracks, some lanes, no stiles
**LANDSCAPE** Intimate and deep winding valleys, coppiced woodland and heathland **SUGGESTED MAP** OS Explorer 133 Haslemere & Petersfield
**START/FINISH** Grid reference: SU 864315 **DOG FRIENDLINESS** On a lead through Newland Cottage's horse paddocks and along lanes. On Linchmere Common there could be a few Shetland cattle grazing **PARKING** Along the lane through Linchmere Common either side of the Lynchmere Society information board **PUBLIC TOILETS** None on route

## WALK 31 DIRECTIONS

❶ Pass to the left of the Lynchmere Society notice board by the lane onto the footpath across the common, heading towards a kissing gate. Through this continue quarter left to a kissing gate. Leaving the common, continue on a path, a fence to your left. At the end bear right along a lane, leaving it at a cattle grid to continue ahead downhill to skirt to the right of Danley Farm and through a gate.

❷ Continue to a kissing gate on the edge of the wood. Through this follow the footpath posts left, then right, climbing, and bear left to walk within the edge of the woods, beside a valley with Danley Farm at its head. The path then enters the woods, mostly sweet chestnut coppicing. Shortly the path bears left through a bridle gate and you continue ahead to the valley floor.

❸ At a footpath post ignore a gate into a field and bear right, still within the woodland edge. Continue to a footpath post, a pond on your left. Bear left to skirt it and cross a footbridge to continue ahead past fields to reach a lane. Bear right along the lane and where the lane bears left continue ahead, to the right of Corner Cottage. Continue ahead on a track, at first in the edge of woods, then within.

❹ At paddocks go left through a gate at the end of the first paddock and before reaching Newland Cottage.

Descend to go through another onto a footbridge and out through a third gate. Continue ahead along the edge of a fir plantation, then within it. At a path junction bear left and at the crest bear right at the footpath post and follow the path, eventually crossing a footbridge before reaching a lane.

❺ Here bear left and pass Shulbrede Priory. Continue uphill, then down to a bridge. Cross the bridge and almost immediately bear half right at the footpath post into the woods. At a drive bear right, then left to follow it left uphill, passing to the left of a garage. Now on a path within woods climb to the crest and continue, a silver birch copse on your right. At a footpath junction bear left and climb towards the road.

❻ Just before the road go right and climb steeply. Levelling out go left at a gate and skirt a cricket ground. Through a gate, continue to the road and bear left to visit Linchmere church. Then retrace your steps and continue ahead to end the walk at the common.

---

### 🍴 EATING AND DRINKING

Liphook, over the border in Hampshire, has a few pubs and a café in the Sainsbury's supermarket near the station. If you prefer a more rural location, the nearest to Linchmere is The Prince of Wales in Hammer Bottom, also in Hampshire. This does good food as well as cask ales.

# VILLAGES OF THE ROTHER VALLEY

An attractive walk along the secluded Rother Valley, returning across fine, sandy heathland.

The historic highlight of this walk is Trotton's St George's parish church, not for the exterior but for the interior. Aisleless, the nave west wall and parts of other walls have 14th-century wall paintings. These had been preserved by Protestant whitewash removed in a 1904 restoration. The nave west wall has a vast Last Judgement with Christ in Majesty at the top and a horned Moses below. To the right is the Good Man surrounded by the seven Acts of Mercy and to the left side is a fading Evil Man surrounded by the Seven Deadly Sins. There are also other figures and unclear paintings on the north and south walls, those above the south door seem to be members of the Camoys family who held the manor in the 14th century, judging by the arms on the shields above the kneeling figures.

More famous, though, is the brass to Thomas, Lord Camoys, and his wife in the chancel, one of the biggest, best-preserved and most ornate brasses to survive in England. Affixed to one of the three table tombs at the east end, the brass of about 1419 has Lord Camoys in full armour holding hands with Elizabeth, his second wife. Thomas led the left wing of the English army at the great victory of Agincourt under Henry V in 1415. He was made a Knight of the Garter by the King soon after, and you can see the garter just below his left knee on the brass. Also there is the earliest known brass to a female, Margaret, Lady Camoys who died in 1310.

Behind the church is Trotton Place, which was built in about 1600 but was encased and altered in the early 18th century. This is the brick façade and dormer windowed hipped slate roof seen as you approach Trotton on the opposite side of the river.

### Iping and Trotton Commons

These sandy heaths were used in the past for furze, firewood and grazing by the villagers, but after this stopped in the 1930s scrub, birch and bracken took over. Gradually the heathland is being restored and grazed by a small number of cattle and there is now more heather and less bracken. The nightjar is back and with luck you might see one or two sweeping the skies at dusk.

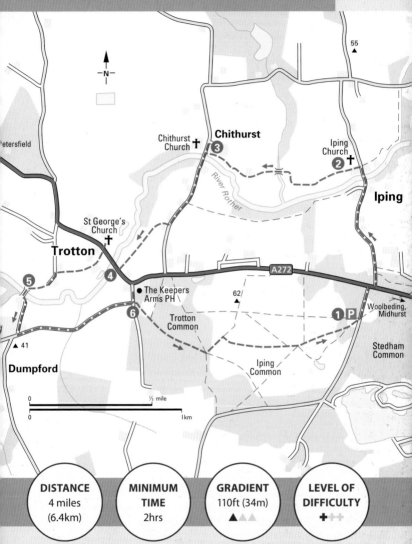

| DISTANCE | MINIMUM TIME | GRADIENT | LEVEL OF DIFFICULTY |
|---|---|---|---|
| 4 miles (6.4km) | 2hrs | 110ft (34m) ▲▲▲ | +++ |

**PATHS** Tracks and paths across heathland, field paths and some lanes, 12 stiles

**LANDSCAPE** Heathland and fields along a river valley

**SUGGESTED MAP** OS Explorer 133 Haslemere & Petersfield

**START/FINISH** Grid reference: SU 852220

**DOG FRIENDLINESS** On a lead along roads and lanes and amid cattle and horses along the Rother between Iping and Trotton

**PARKING** Iping Common Car Park accessed off the A272

**PUBLIC TOILETS** None on route

*Opposite: Heathland on Iping Common*

## WALK 32 DIRECTIONS

❶ From the car park bear left along the lane, cross the A272 and follow the lane downhill into Iping. Cross the River Rother for the first time over the partly 17th-century bridge and go left into the churchyard via a gate.

❷ Leave the churchyard at its far corner via a stile. Continue half left across horse pasture towards a stile by a field gate. Continue along the field edge, then through a tree belt with a stream via an elegant metal footbridge, a stile at each end, to continue ahead to a stile to the left of a stone field barn. Over this continue into the far corner of a tapering field. Out over a stile, onto a track and over another stile bear left onto a track and reach a lane.

❸ Bear right to visit the unspoiled and simple 11th-century Chithurst church on its mound overlooking the Rother. Then cross the Rother on a mossy stone bridge to follow the lane to a footpath post just past White's Farm. Bear right to a stile and continue ahead to another stile, a view of Trotton Place beyond the river. Over it bear

left alongside a fence, descending to a stile to the left of a rectangular pond. Through a copse and out over a stile cross to another and out onto the A272.

❹ Bear right and cross the Rother over the mainly 15th-century five-arched bridge. Bear right to visit St George's Church with its fine wall paintings and brass memorials. Back to the main road, cross to the telephone kiosk and walk along a gravelled lane. Through a metal kissing gate the lane bears right, by outbuildings, then ahead alongside a post and wire fence. Through a field gate bear half right to a footbridge, bearing left to a bridle gate near Terwick Mill.

❺ Cross the Rother weir on a footbridge and, past the mill buildings, bear left along a lane, passing cottages, to a T-junction. Here bear left and follow the lane and descend to The Keepers Arms for refreshment. Retrace your steps and shortly continue ahead at the footpath sign onto the Serpent's Trail, the road bearing right.

❻ Bear left at a track fork and ascend a sunken lane, then continue onto Trotton Common. At the crest bear left at a footpath post, still on the Serpent's Trail. At a path junction bear right and descend along the track, now on Iping Common. Converging with a track from the right continue ahead, then converge with another track to follow the Serpent's Trail back to the car park.

> ### 🍴 EATING AND DRINKING
> The Keepers Arms at Trotton, an attractive partly tile-hung and whitewashed old building, is a fine pub restaurant with high-quality food. If anything it caters for meals rather than bar snacks, but has a cosy bar and restaurant.

# MEANDERING AROUND MIDHURST

A host of delights awaits on this town and country walk, which follows the pretty River Rother to the ruins of Cowdray House.

Look around you on this walk around Midhurst and you'll spot the yellow paintwork of houses owned by the Cowdray Estate. The grounds of Cowdray Park are famous for polo matches – an important part of the sporting calendar. Not so well known are the majestic ruins of Cowdray House, seen from the car park at the start of the walk and visited just before you finish it.

### Through Midhurst

Begin the walk by embarking on a town trail. It's an easy stroll through the old market town of Midhurst with plenty to see along the way. Old photographs of the town taken in the early part of the 20th century show the part-16th-century Angel Hotel and the building which now houses Barclays Bank. The famous tile-hung library has been preserved too, and the medieval interior is certainly worth looking at. Built in the early part of the 16th century, the building was thought originally to have been a store house or granary. This part of Midhurst is known as Knockhundred Row. The delightfully evocative name is thought to date back to the time when Midhurst had a castle, and the owner could exercise his right to summon 100 men to defend the castle by knocking on the doors of 100 households in the town.

The road passes the old chemist shop where H G Wells worked before attending Midhurst Grammar School. His mother was housekeeper at nearby Uppark House. In the middle of the street, flanked by striking houses and shop fronts, lies the war memorial on which the names of several regiments are recorded. Follow the road to the imposing parish church of St Mary Magdalen and St Denys, which is mostly 19th century but with earlier traces.

The walk, ideal for a summer's evening, eventually leaves Midhurst and heads for rolling, wooded countryside. But it's not long before you are returning to the town, following a path running through woodland above the Rother. Here you can step between the trees on the right to look down at the river and across to Cowdray House. This vista is one of the highlights of the walk, a moment to savour on the homeward leg. The walk finishes by following the Queen's Path, a favourite walk of Elizabeth I.

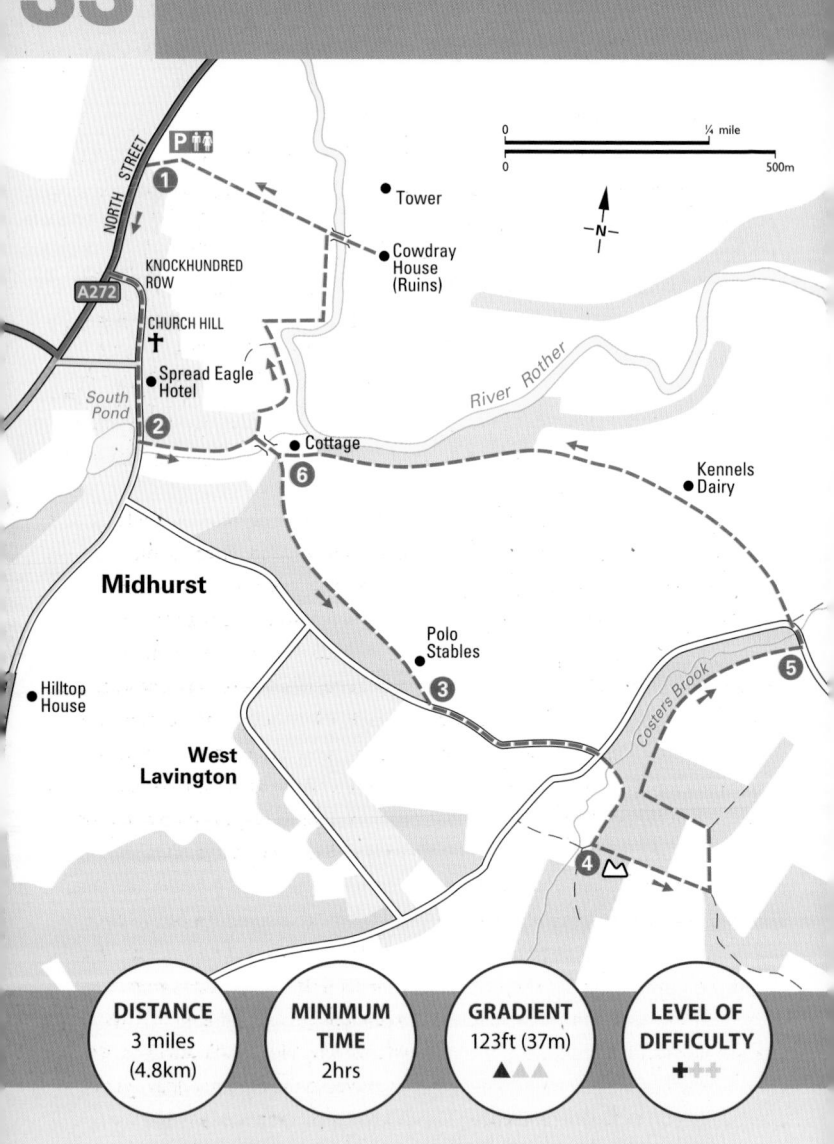

NORTH STREET

Tower

Cowdray
House
(Ruins)

KNOCKHUNDRED
ROW

A272

CHURCH HILL

Spread Eagle
Hotel

South
Pond

River Rother

Cottage

Kennels
Dairy

**Midhurst**

Polo
Stables

Hilltop
House

Costers Brook

**West
Lavington**

## DISTANCE
3 miles
(4.8km)

## MINIMUM TIME
2hrs

## GRADIENT
123ft (37m)
▲▲▲

## LEVEL OF DIFFICULTY
✚✚✚

**PATHS** Pavements, field, riverside tracks and country road, 4 stiles
**LANDSCAPE** Midhurst town and its beautiful rural setting on the Rother
**SUGGESTED MAP** OS Explorer 120 Chichester, South Harting & Selsey
**START/FINISH** Grid reference: SU 886217 **DOG FRIENDLINESS** Off lead on tracks
and stretches of riverside. On lead on roads and busy streets in Midhurst town
centre **PARKING** Car park by tourist information centre in North Street
**PUBLIC TOILETS** Car park and elsewhere in Midhurst

## WALK 33 DIRECTIONS

**1** From the car park by the tourist information centre turn left and walk along North Street, passing the post office. Bear left into Knockhundred Row. Walk along Church Hill and into South Street to pass along the side of the historic Spread Eagle Hotel.

**2** Turn left by South Pond into The Wharf, following a bridleway beside industrial buildings and flats. Trees on the right enclose a stream. Bear right at the next waymarked junction, cross the bridge and pass a cottage on the left. Keep the wooden fencing on the right and avoid the path running off to the left. Make for a stile, then continue ahead along the edge of fields, keeping trees and vegetation on the right. Cross two stiles and follow the path to the right of the polo stables.

**3** Keep left and follow a pleasantly wooded stretch of road. Pass some pretty cottages and on reaching a bend join a bridle path signposted 'Heyshott and Graffham'. Follow the track as it curves to the right.

**4** Veer left just before the entrance to a house and follow the waymarked path as it climbs quite steeply through the trees, passing between woodland glades and bracken. Drop down the slope to a waymarked path junction and turn left to join a sandy track. Keep left at the fork and follow the track as it bends sharply to the right.

> **⊕ EATING AND DRINKING**
>
> Midhurst has several pubs and hotels – among them the Angel in North Street. This extended Tudor coaching inn has a brasserie, set lunches through the week and light snacks in the more informal surroundings of the bar. The Coffee Pot in Knockhundred Row and Ye Olde Tea Shoppe in North Street all offer tea, coffee and lunches.

**5** On reaching the road, turn left and, when it bends left by some gates, go straight on along the bridleway towards Kennels Dairy. Keep to the left of the outbuildings and stable blocks and walk ahead to several galvanised gates. Continue on the path and when it reaches a field gateway, go through the gate to the right of it, following the path as it runs just inside the woodland.

**6** Continue along to the junction, forming part of the outward leg of the walk, turn right and retrace your steps to the bridge. Avoid the path on the left, running along to South Pond, and veer over to the right to rejoin the river bank. Keep going until you reach a footpath on the left, leading up to the ruins of St Ann's Hill. Follow the path beside the Rother, heading for a kissing gate. Turn left and make for a bridge which provides access to Cowdray House. After visiting the house, go straight ahead along the causeway path to the car park.

The Tudor Cowdray House

# GOOD GOING AT GLORIOUS GOODWOOD

This woodland walk past Goodwood Racetrack includes an optional spur to the Weald and Downland Open Air Museum.

Think of horse racing on the South Downs and you immediately think of Goodwood, without doubt one of Britain's loveliest and most famous racecourses. Its superb position, high on the Downs, amid beechwoods, draws crowds from far and wide, and for one week every summer it becomes 'Glorious Goodwood' when thousands of racegoers travel to Sussex to attend one of the most prestigious events of the sporting and social calendar. According to The Times, Goodwood is 'the place to be and to be seen'.

The course opened in 1801 after the Duke of Richmond gave part of his estate to establish a track where members of the Goodwood Hunt Club and officers of the Sussex Militia could attend meetings. However, towards the end of the 19th century the racecourse acquired a rather unfortunate reputation when the rector of Singleton protested to the Chief Constable about the rowdy behaviour of racegoers.

### Hunt with Tradition

The walk begins at Goodwood Country Park, a popular amenity area characterised by woodland and downland grass, and initially follows part of the Monarch's Way through extensive woodland, down to the village of East Dean. Along the road is neighbouring Charlton, famous for the Charlton Hunt. Established in the 18th century, the hunt's most memorable chase took place on 28th January 1738, beginning before eight that morning and not finishing until nearly six that evening. Many of those taking part were from the elite, upper ranks of society and for ten hours that day a fox led the pack a merry dance in the surrounding fields and woods. Eventually, the hounds cornered their prey, an elderly vixen, near the River Arun.

If time allows, you may want to extend the walk and visit the Weald and Downland Museum, with its collection of traditional homes and workplaces. The main walk finishes by skirting Goodwood and on race days crowds line the bridleway alongside it, watching as camera crews dash back and forth in an effort to capture the best television images. The sound of the PA system floats across the course as you witness all the colourful activity.

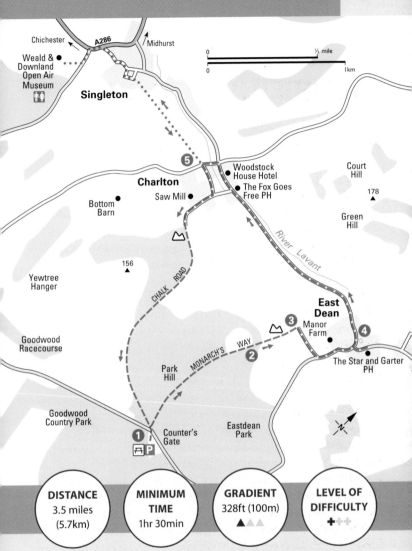

Weald & Downland Open Air Museum

**Singleton**

½ mile

1 km

Woodstock House Hotel

Court Hill

**Charlton**

The Fox Goes Free PH

Saw Mill

178

Bottom Barn

Green Hill

River Lavant

156

CHALK ROAD

Yewtree Hanger

**East Dean**

Manor Farm

Goodwood Racecourse

MONARCH'S WAY

The Star and Garter PH

Park Hill

Goodwood Country Park

Eastdean Park

Counter's Gate

N

---

| DISTANCE | MINIMUM TIME | GRADIENT | LEVEL OF DIFFICULTY |
|---|---|---|---|
| 3.5 miles (5.7km) | 1hr 30min | 328ft (100m) ▲▲ ▲ | ✚ ✚ ✚ |

**PATHS** Woodland tracks and field paths, section of Monarch's Way and one lengthy stretch of quiet road, 4 stiles **LANDSCAPE** Mixture of dense woodland and scenic downland **SUGGESTED MAPS** OS Explorer 120 Chichester, South Harting & Selsey or 121 Arundel & Pulborough **START/FINISH** Grid reference: SU 897113 (on Explorer 120) **DOG FRIENDLINESS** Can run free on woodland tracks **PARKING** Counter's Gate free car park and picnic area at Goodwood Country Park or large free car park opposite racecourse **PUBLIC TOILETS** Weald and Downland Open Air Museum

## WALK 34 DIRECTIONS

❶ Make for the western end of Counter's Gate car park and look for a footpath sign by an opening leading out to the road. Cross over to a junction of two tracks, with a path on the right. Follow the right-hand track, signposted 'public footpath' and part of the Monarch's Way, to a gate and stile. Continue to the next gate and stile and then cross a clearing in the woods.

❷ Cut through this remote, thickly wooded country, following the gently curving path over the grassy, plant-strewn ground and down between trees to a gateway. The village of East Dean can be seen below. Head diagonally right down the steep field slope to reach a stile in the corner.

❸ Cross into the adjacent field and follow the boundary to a second stile leading out to the road. Bear left and walk down into East Dean, passing Manor Farm. Keep right at the junction in the village centre.

❹ Leave East Dean by keeping the pond on your right-hand side and follow the road towards Midhurst and Singleton. On reaching Charlton

### ⬤ IN THE AREA
Visit the Weald and Downland Open Air Museum which is set in 50 acres (20ha) of Sussex countryside, the museum offers a collection of over 40 regional historic buildings which have been saved from destruction, painstakingly restored and rebuilt.

village, pass The Fox Goes Free pub and the Woodstock House Hotel and take the next left turning. Follow the lane to a stile on the right and a turning on the left. To visit the Open Air Museum at Singleton, cross over into the fields and follow the straight path. Return to this stile by the same route and take the road opposite.

❺ Walk along to the junction and turn right by the war memorial, dedicated to fallen comrades of the Sussex Yeomanry in both World Wars. Follow Chalk Road which dwindles to a track on the outskirts of Charlton. Once clear of the village, the track climbs steadily between the trees. On the left are glimpses of a rolling landscape, while to the right the racecourse edges into view. Follow the track all the way to the road and cross to return to the car park.

### 🍴 EATING AND DRINKING
The Star and Garter at East Dean and the 400-year-old Fox Goes Free at Charlton both offer a good range of meals and snacks and enjoy a very pleasant South Downs setting. There is a café at the Weald and Downland Open Air Museum, offering hot soup, filled rolls, quiche, Cornish pasties, cakes and pastries.

# A SUSSEX SECRET

A stroll focused on one of Sussex's finest but surprisingly little-known churches, once a medieval priory.

Situated east of the village street in a peaceful and pretty setting, Boxgrove Priory is to many probably the finest parish church in Sussex. It is not in one of the most scenic parts of Sussex, being on the coastal plain and between two busy roads but those who divert to the village will find the Priory worthwhile.

The medieval priory church has considerable historic and architectural interest. Its chief glory is the choir or eastern arm, which was rebuilt very soon after 1200, replacing a smaller Norman one. On a sumptuous scale the new choir took the choir of Portsmouth Cathedral of the 1190s as its model and developed the design of two arches enclosed within a larger one. Elegant stone-ribbed roof vaults soar above and the arcades make judicious use of Purbeck marble from Dorset for columns, shafts and capitals. You will see that the columns get more elegant and airy as you approach the high altar.

The priory was founded around 1115 as a cell of Lessay Abbey in the Cotentin peninsula of Normandy. The founder was the lord of nearby Halnaker, Robert de la Haye, whose family also came from near Lessay. From his building the transepts and first bays of the nave survive as well as the chapter house west wall to the north. The nave beyond the Norman bays was built later in the 12th century, but demolished after the Priory was dissolved in 1536, the parishioners fortunately moving into the vacated monastic choir.

## 'A Poor Chapel'

The choir was saved thanks to Thomas De La Warr of Halnaker whose chantry had only been built within the choir aisle four years before in 1532. Indeed a surviving letter from De La Warr to Thomas Cromwell begs that 'his power (poor) chapel to be buried yn' and the choir be spared demolition'. So while you admire the choir also admire the chantry chapel in the south choir aisle that in effect saved this wonderful church from destruction.

The choir vaults were painted with heraldic shields intertwined in foliage. The artist was Lambert Barnard, probably commissioned by Thomas in the 1530s. Barnard is better known for the huge 1520s panels in Chichester Cathedral depicting the kings of England and the bishops of Chichester.

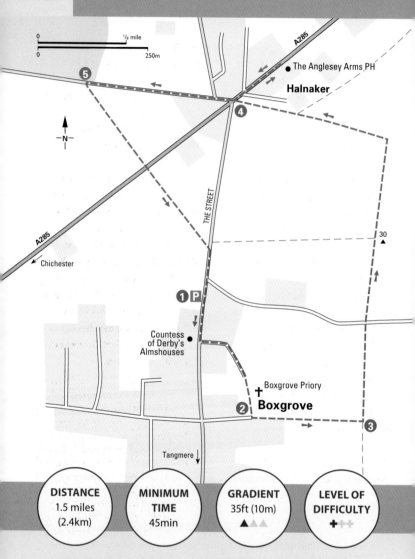

The Anglesey Arms PH

**Halnaker**

A285

THE STREET

A285

← Chichester

30 ▲

① P

Countess
of Derby's
Almshouses

✝ Boxgrove Priory

② **Boxgrove**

③

Tangmere ↓

| DISTANCE | MINIMUM TIME | GRADIENT | LEVEL OF DIFFICULTY |
|---|---|---|---|
| 1.5 miles (2.4km) | 45min | 35ft (10m) ▲▲▲ | ✚✚✚ |

**PATHS** Field tracks and paths, some roads and a village street, no stiles
**LANDSCAPE** The Sussex coastal plain, relatively flat and a mix of arable
and pasture **SUGGESTED MAP** OS Explorer 121 Arundel & Pulborough
**START/FINISH** Grid reference: SU 906076
**DOG FRIENDLINESS** On a lead in Boxgrove and at Halnaker, particularly crossing
the busy A285 **PARKING** Boxgrove Village Hall car park, The Street, Boxgrove
**PUBLIC TOILETS** None on route

## WALK 35 DIRECTIONS

❶ From the car park bear right along the village street a short way, then, opposite the 18th-century almshouses bear left, signed 'Boxgrove Priory', along a metalled track between flint and brick walls. The track bears right. On the left are the ruins of the 14th-century priory guest house that you can visit via a gate. After this go through a hedge gap to pass in front of the chapter house front wall with its three Norman arches. Then go through a gate and bear left through an archway to visit the priory, entering it through the south porch.

❷ Leave the priory church via the south gate and bear left through a kissing gate to walk alongside the churchyard's flint boundary wall. Continue ahead across a field, Halnaker's restored 18th-century windmill away to the left.

❸ At a footpath post bear left along a field track, a large field to your right. Continue ahead past a footpath post,

now on a path and pass two further footpath signposts, mainly within a staggered avenue of young trees, mostly rowan, lime and ash. The path bears left and, reaching a footpath fork, take the left fork. Through a kissing gate you reach the road.

❹ Go right, heading towards a flint archway, the early 19th-century south-east gateway to the Goodwood Estate. The main road follows the course of the old Roman road from London to Chichester, Stane (stone or paved) Street. Here you can divert right to visit The Anglesey Arms. Whether you divert or not, cross the main road to the flint archway and bear left along the lane, a view of Chichester Cathedral's spire ahead.

> ### 🍴 EATING AND DRINKING
>
> Within Boxgrove village there is Boxgrove Village Stores and Post Office for iron rations, snacks and cold drinks. In Halnaker village, near Point ❹, The Anglesey Arms does good food and a 'seasonal lunch time menu at the bar', which means well-cooked bar meals.

> ### 🌀 IN THE AREA
>
> About a mile (1.6km) south of the A27 Arundel to Chichester road roundabout visit Tangmere Military Aviation Museum. There has been an airfield here since 1916 but its glory days were during the Second World War and the museum tells the airfield's history and has a fine collection of aircraft.

❺ At a footpath sign go left through a gate and continue half left towards another gate across the field. Through this gate cross the main road, the ruins of the priory guest house and the church tower ahead. Continue along a grassy path and at The Street bear right into the car park.

# A ROMAN AND MEDIEVAL TOWN

A town stroll focused on Chichester's walls and medieval
past as well as its 19th-century canal heritage.

Occupying most of the city's south-west quadrant, the cathedral and its close
dominate the city, the cathedral tower and spire soaring to 269ft (82m). The
original see was transferred to Chichester after the Norman Conquest and
work started on the cathedral in the 1080s within the town's old Roman walls.

A dedication took place in 1108, probably with the choir and transepts
completed and work finished in the 1140s. A disastrous fire in 1187 that also
destroyed much of the city led to a new east end, refacing of the interior walls
and a fireproof stone vaulted roof. The spire was added in about 1400.

Towers fell throughout the cathedral's history, two in 1210 storms, one in
the 1630s but the most spectacular one was just in the age of photography. In
1861 the central tower collapsed and the aftermath recorded. The tower and
spire were rebuilt by Sir George Gilbert Scott.

## A City Girdled

A remarkable amount of the city walls that surrounded the Roman and
medieval city survive. In three of the 'quadrants' you can walk along them on
promenades built in the 18th century and look over the city and its environs.
The Georgians also refaced the walls with flints and it is now difficult to see
much older material. The city walls were built around AD200 with bastions
added in the 4th century AD. As well as medieval improvement and additions
four gatehouses were built, the last only demolished in the late 18th century
for road improvement.

## Canal Basin

The Chichester Ship Canal was an attempt to improve city trade and the
4-mile long (6.4km) canal was built to carry ships of up to a 100 tons from
the sea to the city through the Chichester Canal. The canal opened in 1822
but was effectively killed off by the railways and finally closed to commerce
around 1906. The basin has a converted warehouse, a customs house cottage
and a waterside pub but there are also some modern buildings and it is hard
to imagine it in its heyday.

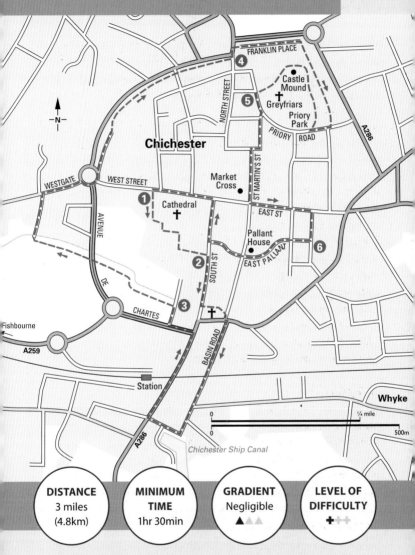

| DISTANCE | MINIMUM TIME | GRADIENT | LEVEL OF DIFFICULTY |
|---|---|---|---|
| 3 miles (4.8km) | 1hr 30min | Negligible ▲▲▲ | ✚✚✚ |

**PATHS** City streets and lanes, town wall walks and parks, no stiles
**LANDSCAPE** The City of Chichester within and without the city walls
**SUGGESTED MAP** OS Explorer 120 Chichester, South Harting & Selsey
**START/FINISH** Grid reference: SU 859047 **DOG FRIENDLINESS** On a lead throughout this walk **PARKING** There are many car parks to choose in the city, mostly free on Sundays **PUBLIC TOILETS** At the cathedral at the start, and on the route in both Northgate Car Park and Priory Park

## WALK 36 DIRECTIONS

**❶** Start outside the cathedral by the statue of St Richard of Chichester. Go past the cathedral entrance and through an archway into the cloisters, then right at the sign for the Palace Gardens into St Richard's Walk. At the end bear left along Canon Lane and leave through the medieval gatehouse.

**❷** Turn right into South Street and then go left along Old Market Avenue. Past Christ Church bear right and cross at the pedestrian lights to continue ahead across the railway on Basin Road to the Chichester Ship Canal basin. Pass the Waterside Inn and bear right to cross the railway again, this time by the station. Cross the ring road at the pedestrian lights and bear left, then right alongside the car park bridge.

**❸** At the end of the car park bridge bear left along a gravelled walk, the city walls to your right. Cross the ring road, the Avenue de Chartres, and continue alongside a post and rail fence, going right at the end onto a foot and cycle path over a footbridge. At the road, Westgate, bear right to a roundabout. Go left at the sign 'Walls Walk' and cross West Street and into North Walls Lane. Shortly ascend to the wall walk that takes you along the city wall's north-west quadrant to descend into North Street at the end.

**❹** Bear left into North Street, then right to walk along Franklin Place, a long row of stucco early 19th-century cottages. At the end bear right and walk through a park, the city walls alongside. At the road (Priory Road) bear right, then right again into Priory Park via a gate. Immediately bear right and ascend to walk along the city walls walk. Descend and through a gate walk up onto the castle mound, which gives a good view of the 1270s Greyfriars church, before leaving the park via the west gate.

> **🍽 EATING AND DRINKING**
> There is plenty of choice of pubs, restaurants and cafés in the city. These range from The Buttery At The Crypt in South Street to the Waterside Inn by the canal basin.

**❺** Back on Priory Road, follow it to The Park Tavern and continue into St Martin's Square and pass the medieval St Mary's Hospital. Continue down St Martin's Street past the Hole in the Wall pub and at the end bear left into East Street. Continue past the Doric portico of the former corn exchange and go right into St John's Street.

**❻** Bear right into New Town and continue ahead at the crossroads into East Pallant, a fine run of Georgian town houses. At the Pallant crossroads on your right is Pallant House, now an art gallery. Continue along West Pallant to South Street and bear right towards Bishop Story's Market Cross of 1501 and left here back to the cathedral.

# UP TO
# UP MARDEN

A walk on the Downs to and from one of Sussex's
most unspoiled medieval churches.

Up on the downs are three small churches, in the tiny hamlets of East Marden,
North Marden and Up Marden. The biggest village is West Marden, where
this walk starts, which grew up in a valley at right angles to the main road
to Petersfield but this has no church (it was deconsecrated before 1585 and
demolished soon after). This walk climbs to Up Marden, the best of the three,
but the other two churches are well worth a visit. East Marden is a plain 13th-
century church with lancet windows, a feature of interest being the chamber
organ that was once Prince Albert's. North Marden is a simple Norman
church, in effect a room with an apsidal or semi-circular east end and a rare
example of a single 'cell' or single roomed church with such an apse, such
small Norman churches usually being square ended.

## Up Marden's Unspoiled Church
This fine and atmospheric church is on the edge of a dry valley in a settlement
first mentioned in a charter in about 930 as a place 'which the yokels call
Upmerdon'. The Church of St Michael is whitewashed inside on uneven wall
plaster with irregular brick and stone flag floors; all the window glass is clear.

The church has escaped heavy-handed restoration. The wagon roof has
not had its plaster removed to expose the rafters as was a normal Victorian
improvement. The simple Georgian pews remain in the chancel, along
with the turned baluster altar rails and the font is a simple stone bowl on a
shaft. There are a few Georgian wall memorial tablets to local gentry and
the Victorians added pews to the nave as well as the candelabra and the
surprisingly suitable stone pulpit. All in all, the church is a textbook example
of how not to strip away the love and care and accretions of countless
generations of worshippers since construction in the 13th century.

However, some whitewash has been removed to expose wall paintings
including a 14th-century St Nicholas carrying the young Christ and what
appears to be consecration crosses in some window jambs. All this, though,
adds to the building's interest, charm and unspoiled atmosphere, isolated in
a grassy churchyard high up on the Downs.

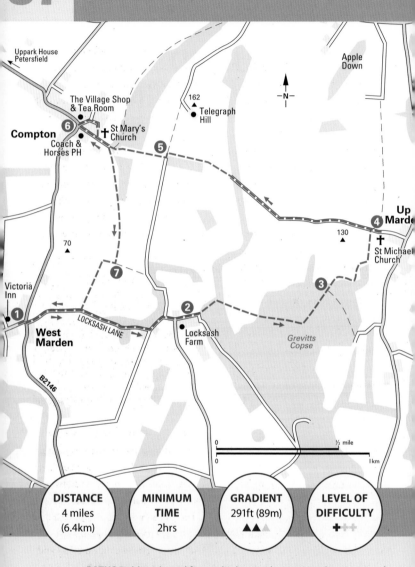

Uppark House
Petersfield →

Apple
Down

The Village Shop
& Tea Room

162
▲ Telegraph
Hill

**Compton** **6**

✝ St Mary's
Church

**5**

Coach &
Horses PH

Up
Marden **4**

✝ St Michael
Church

70
▲

130
▲

**3**

Victoria
Inn

**7**

**1**

LOCKSASH LANE

West
Marden

**2**

Locksash
Farm

Grevitts
Copse

B2146

0                          ½ mile

0                          1 km

—N—

## DISTANCE
4 miles
(6.4km)

## MINIMUM TIME
2hrs

## GRADIENT
291ft (89m)
▲▲▲

## LEVEL OF DIFFICULTY
✛✛✛

**PATHS** Field tracks and footpaths, lane at the start, 5 stiles

**LANDSCAPE** Rolling chalk downland and dry valleys, some woodland

**SUGGESTED MAP** OS Explorer 120 Chichester, South Harting & Selsey

**START/FINISH** Grid reference: SU 771135

**DOG FRIENDLINESS** On a lead on the lanes and in the villages

**PARKING** Roadside parking in West Marden village

**PUBLIC TOILETS** None on route

## WALK 37 DIRECTIONS

**1** From West Marden cross the B2146 and continue along Locksash Lane, Uppark House away to your left. Climb and follow the lane as it bears left past a brick and flint cottage to Locksash Farm. Continue to the left of the farm buildings and pass a footpath post.

**2** The track descends to a fork, the footpath continuing straight ahead into the woods. Descend to a stile amid old hazel coppicing. Beyond, bear half right to the field-edge, then continueahead across the valley floor field. Over the stile continue ahead through the wood, Grevitts Copse. Shortly the track bears quarter left, now passing through a sweet chestnut coppice and bearing gently left to the crest. Continue ahead at footpath post and descend, continuing ahead at a footpath junction post to a stile.

**3** Over the stile and out of the woods bear right along the field-edge and follow the field-edge as it bears left, right and left again all the way to a track, with occasional glimpses of Up Marden church through the hedge. At the track bear right uphill and then go right into Up Marden churchyard to visit this delightful downland church.

**4** Return to the track and bear left, initially retracing your steps before continuing on the track downhill to cross a dry valley. At a footpath post continue, now on a footpath rather

than a track, which shortly widens into a green lane descending steeply to the valley floor. Continue as the path climbs out of the valley to pass through a tree belt then beside a conifer copse.

**5** At a track bear left, then shortly bear right to a stile by a field entrance. Bear right alongside the hedge to descend steeply towards Compton to a stile. Over this bear half right to join the track to descend into Compton village.

---

### 🍴 EATING AND DRINKING

Very popular with walkers The Village Shop and Tea Room in Compton is open nearly every day, the tea room closing at 4.30. There are two pubs, the Coach and Horses in Compton and the Victoria Inn in West Marden and both do rather pricier food.

---

**6** At Compton's village centre, bear right to the church. From the church go along the path alongside flint buildings and leave the churchyard via steps and back into School Lane, the route by which you entered the village. Bear left and retrace your steps uphill. As the path bears right take the right fork and continue climbing out of the valley on the bridleway, levelling out at the crest.

**7** Reaching a track junction, go right. Shortly the track bears left and descends steadily to a junction. Here turn right to retrace your steps back to West Marden.

# A TALE OF TWO CANALS

A walk tracing the routes of the Chichester Ship Canal, the Portsmouth and Arundel Canal and the Selsey Tramway.

This route follows sections of two canals: the Chichester Channel to Hunston where it turns north towards the city and the Portsmouth and Arundel Canal, traceable east of Hunston on the walk route.

## The Canals

The canals opened in 1822 and the Chichester Ship Canal ended at the Southgate Canal Basin, south of the railway station in Chichester on the outskirts of the city (Walk 36). In decline from the mid-19th century, the last commercial cargo was six tons of ballast delivered to Chichester in 1906.

The Portsmouth and Arundel Canal didn't fare as well. Built by the Portsmouth and Arundel Navigation Company it offered a safe inland route. However by the time it was built the Napoleonic Wars were over and the coastal trade preferred the cheaper open sea routes. Nowadays some stretches have a little water, other stretches have entirely been filled in but the stretch between Hunston and Runcton is one of the better ones. Here, you can glimpse water in the reedy and tree-screened canal, for example by the pedestrian lights in North Mundham.

## The Selsey Tramway

More usually known as the Selsey Tramway or, unofficially and less flatteringly, 'the Siddlesham Snail', and the West Sussex Railway, this was one of those light railway lines built by Colonel Stephens who was also responsible for the Kent and East Sussex Railway seen from Bodiam on Walk 4. Like that one it used converted buses with railway wheels as well as wheezy old tank engines.

The tramway opened in 1897 and crossed the Chichester Canal by a lifting bridge, the abutments of which remain and were recently repaired. The line continued south from the canal along the footpath and beyond Point ❹ to head across the flat coastal plain to Selsey. It was closed in 1935, having sustained irrevocable damage to its finances in floods that in 1910 washed away the southern section of the line at Sidlesham (Walk 39). It was also unable to cope with competition from local buses.

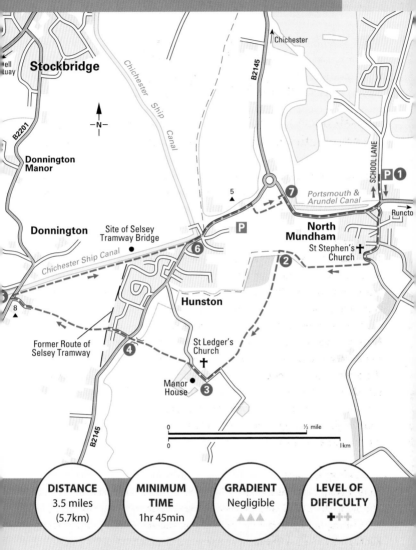

Stockbridge

Chichester

Chichester Ship Canal

B2145

SCHOOL LANE

P 1

Donnington Manor

B2201

N

Portsmouth & Arundel Canal

7

Runcto

Donnington

Site of Selsey Tramway Bridge

P

North Mundham

St Stephen's Church

Chichester Ship Canal

6

2

Hunston

3

8

Former Route of Selsey Tramway

4

St Ledger's Church

Manor House

3

0    ½ mile

0    1km

B2145

**DISTANCE**
3.5 miles
(5.7km)

**MINIMUM TIME**
1hr 45min

**GRADIENT**
Negligible
▲▲▲

**LEVEL OF DIFFICULTY**
✚✚✚

**PATHS** Field tracks and footpaths, canal tow path and lanes, 2 stiles
**LANDSCAPE** Sussex Coastal plain, mainly arable and market gardening, and canal side **SUGGESTED MAP** OS Explorer 120 Chichester, South Harting & Selsey **START/FINISH** Grid reference: SU 875026
**DOG FRIENDLINESS** On a lead on the lanes and in the villages
**PARKING** North Mundham Playing Fields car park, School Lane
**PUBLIC TOILETS** None on route

## WALK 38 DIRECTIONS

❶ From the car park walk back up School Lane to the main road and cross via the pedestrian lights into Church Road. Follow the road curving right and pass the lychgate to North Mundham church. Shortly bear right onto a footpath. Go through a kissing gate and keep ahead, following the hedge as it bears right, then left.

❷ Go left at a footpath sign and alongside the left side of a wood, a field on your left. At the end of the wood continue through a hedge gap now on a farm track. Pass a paddock and bear right at footpath sign onto a path that becomes a gravelled lane.

❸ On the right is St Ledger's Church and on the left beyond a reed fringed pond is the Manor House, built about 1680. Just beyond the pond bear left at a footpath post and immediately right to continue alongside a post and wire fence. Through a hedge gap, go left along the edge of playing fields, left of a play area and over a footbridge.

### 🍴 EATING AND DRINKING

There are no pubs or shops on the route. The nearest is The Walnut Tree at the Runcton crossroads roundabout about 500yds (470m) east of North Mundham. This is a pub restaurant with a good 'Lite Bite' lunch menu. In Hunston along the B2145 there is The Spotted Cow pub where you can eat in or get take away fish and chips.

❹ Cross the B2145 Selsey Road, and continue ahead into Little Boultons. The track you cross just before the stile is the trackbed of the Selsey Tramway. Over the stile continue ahead and at a hedge gap go right, then bear left along the farm track through arable fields towards farm buildings ahead. At the farm continue ahead to the right of a conifer hedge to a stile. Over this continue to the road.

❺ Bear right along the road and just before a bridge bear right onto the tow path of the Chichester Ship Canal. Reaching housing you'll see the abutments of the former bridge by which the Selsey Tramway crossed the canal, while the footpath behind the houses continues along its trackbed. Where the Chichester Canal bears left take the path to the road.

❻ At the road cross over and bear left, shortly with a hedge between the pavement and the road. At the end the path bears right, leaving the road and shortly bearing left, this path is also a cycle way. After it bears left again bear right onto a footpath.

❼ At the road bear right back along the road into North Mundham, the Portsmouth and Arundel Canal remnants along the north side of the road amid the trees. Cross Church Road and at the pedestrian lights, the canal now behind you, cross into School Lane and the car park.

# WATERMILLS AND TIDAL MARSHES

A walk along the edge of the tidal marsh
and mudflats of Pagham Harbour.

Until 1919 the tranquil views of Sidlesham Quay seen from the Pagham Harbour side were very different. A large watermill with three waterwheels driving eight pairs of stones occupied the grassy area bounded by the Bembridge limestone quay walls and where a bench now sits. Towering over the adjacent cottages, it was built in 1755 by Benjamin Barlow for Woodruffe Drinkwater and replaced a more modest tide mill. The new mill could grind a whole load of corn in the very fast time, for the 18th century, of one hour.

By the 1870s, Pagham Harbour's trade had declined and the harbour was dammed in 1876 and turned over to agriculture. Without a water supply the mill went out of business, although it attempted to fight back with steam power. Nature took a hand, however, and in the great storms of 1910 the sea broke through the dam, flooding the harbour and surrounding land and washing away a long stretch of the Selsey Tramway. Despite the water coming back it was too late for Sidlesham Mill. It was demolished in 1919 and the large millpond that stretched some 500yds (470m) north of the causeway was drained and is now farmed, apart from the section nearest the causeway of Mill Lane, which is retained as a more modest pond.

### Pagham Harbour

Looking out over the harbour it looks as if it has been tidal mudflats and salt marsh for ever, but it has been subject to numerous unsuccessful attempts to drain it and convert it to farm land, the most recent and apparently successful one being that from 1876 until 1910 when 700 acres (283ha) were reclaimed. After 1910 no further attempts followed and the harbour soon became much as you see it today. It is also protected now as a local nature reserve in which many species of birds have been recorded, as well as marsh plants, and on the shingle ridges further out are rare plants such as the Chidling Pink.

The nature reserve covers 1,500 acres (607 ha) of which about half is intertidal salt marsh and mudflats with shingle, some open water, creeks and wet grassland habitats. Naturally it attracts huge numbers of waders and wildfowl and is an important stop over for migrating birds.

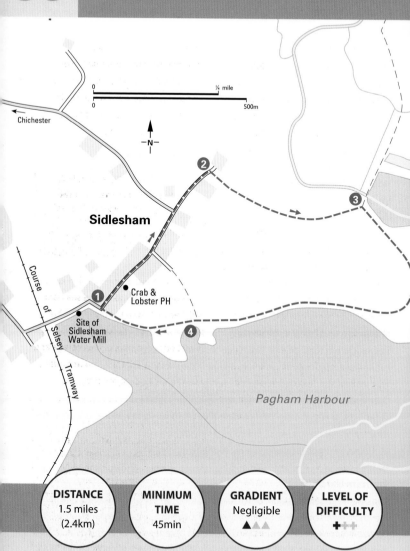

Chichester

¼ mile

500m

—N—

**Sidlesham**

Course of Selsey Tramway

Site of Sidlesham Water Mill

Crab & Lobster PH

*Pagham Harbour*

**DISTANCE**
1.5 miles
(2.4km)

**MINIMUM TIME**
45min

**GRADIENT**
Negligible
▲▲▲

**LEVEL OF DIFFICULTY**
✚✚✚

**PATHS** Lanes, field paths and a coastal path, 4 stiles
**LANDSCAPE** Lush watermeadow cattle pasture and the Pagham Harbour salt marshes and mudflats **SUGGESTED MAP** OS Explorer 120 Chichester, South Harting & Selsey **START/FINISH** Grid reference: SU 861972
**DOG FRIENDLINESS** On a lead on the lane and through the cattle pasture before you reach Pagham Harbour **PARKING** Sidlesham Quay
**PUBLIC TOILETS** None on route

## WALK 39 DIRECTIONS

**❶** From Sidlesham Quay go along the lane past the Crab and Lobster, shortly passing the Old Malthouse dated 1738 – a 'modernisation' of a 16th-century timber-framed cottage. Out of the village where the lane bears left go right and through a hand gate by a sign 'Halsey's Farm Barn' and along a metalled track.

**❷** At a footpath junction bear right over a stile beside a field gate. Continue along a path between hedges. At the end cross a stile into cattle grazed meadows with distant views of the Goodwood racecourse on the South Downs skyline. Continue alongside the hedge and through a hedge gap carry on alongside the hedge. At the far corner of the field climb a stile up to the Pagham Harbour sea bank, Pagham church spire visible on the other side of the harbour ahead.

**❸** Bear right onto the path along the sea bank wall, soon descending to a path alongside, actually on the mudflats, then back onto the bank. Generally speaking follow the path alongside the sea bank wall, sometimes on it, but more often than not alongside. At one point you descend concrete steps to cross a watercourse: be careful they can be very slippery. Eventually, some way on and having curved westward, ignore a permissive path sign on your right.

> **🍴 EATING AND DRINKING**
>
> At Sidlesham Quay there is only one watering hole, the 5-star The Crab and Lobster in Mill Lane. The Anchor in Sidlesham village offers bar meals.

**❹** After passing a footpath sign cross a footbridge and shortly the sea bank wall becomes a sandstone one. The path along the harbour's edge passes Alley Cottage, a slate-hung cottage and then a stone-built former warehouse and you are back at the quay.

> **🦢 ON THE WALK**
>
> As you walk along the edge of Pagham Harbour you might see the little egret, an elegant white bird that is a relation of the heron. These birds first arrived in England in 1989 and first bred in Dorset six years later. Being white they are easily picked out. They breed here and often number over 40 birds at a time.

> **🌿 IN THE AREA**
>
> Immediately beyond the end of the causeway west of Sidlesham Quay the road crosses the course of the Hundred of Manhood and Selsey Tramway that ran along the west edge of Pagham Harbour (Walk 38), the 'Siddlesham Snail'. It was here that the sea broke through in 1910 and washed away Mill Lane station and much of the track. The rebuilding cost prejudiced the future of the line and it closed in 1935.

# WEST ITCHENOR – HARBOUR SAILS AND TRAILS

Chichester Harbour's plentiful wildlife and colourful yachting activity form the backdrop to this fascinating waterside walk.

Weekend sailors flock to Chichester's vast natural harbour, making it one of the most popular attractions on the south coast. The harbour has about 50 miles (80km) of shoreline and 17 miles (27km) of navigable channel, though there is almost no commercial traffic. The Romans cast an approving eye over this impressive stretch of water and established a military base and harbour at nearby Fishbourne after the Claudian invasion of Britain in AD43. Charles II had a fondness for the area too and kept a yacht here.

## Boat Building Legacy

Situated at the confluence of the Bosham and Chichester channels of the estuary is the sailing village of Itchenor, with its main street of picturesque houses and cottages running down to the waterfront. Originally named Icenor, this small settlement started life as a remote, sparsely populated community, but by the 18th century it had begun to play a vital role in the shipbuilding industry. Small warships were built here by the merchants of Chichester, though in later years shipbuilding ceased altogether and any trace of its previous prosperity disappeared beneath the houses and the harbour mud. However, the modern age of leisure and recreation has seen a revival in boat building and yachting, and today Itchenor is once again bustling with boatyards, sailors and chandlers.

## Important Tidal Habitat

But there is much more to Chichester Harbour than sailing. Take a stroll along the harbour edge and you will find there is much to capture the attention. With its intertidal habitats, the harbour is a haven for plant life and wildlife. Wading birds such as curlew, redshank and dunlin can be seen using their differently shaped bills to extract food from the ecologically rich mudflats and terns may be spotted plunging to catch fish. Plants include sea lavender and glasswort, and many of them are able to resist flooding and changing saltiness. Salt marsh is one of the typical habitats of Chichester Harbour and the plants grow in different places according to how often they are flooded.

*Opposite: Sunset at West Itchenor Harbour*

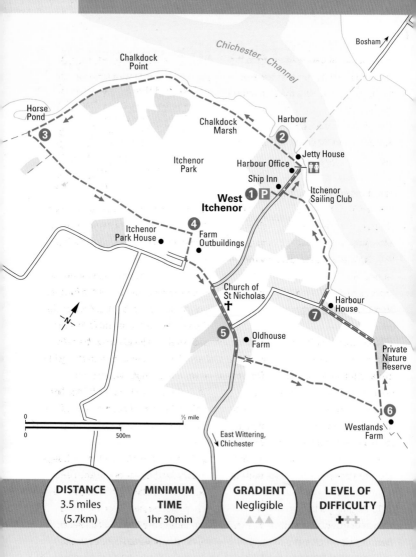

DISTANCE
3.5 miles
(5.7km)

MINIMUM
TIME
1hr 30min

GRADIENT
Negligible
▲▲▲

LEVEL OF
DIFFICULTY
+++

**PATHS** Shoreline, field tracks and paths, 1 stile **LANDSCAPE** Open farmland
and coastal scenery **SUGGESTED MAP** OS Explorer 120 Chichester,
South Harting & Selsey **START/FINISH** Grid reference: SU 797013
**DOG FRIENDLINESS** Waterside paths are ideal for dogs but keep under control
on stretches of open farmland and on short section of road. Dogs permitted on
harbour water tour **PARKING** Large pay-and-display car park in West Itchenor
**PUBLIC TOILETS** West Itchenor